NOTICE

This book is intended as reference material only, not as a medical or legal guide. It is a compilation of the author's experiences, other volunteer participants, and citations from various authors, physicians and authorities in the field of abuse.

If you believe that you are being abused, you should seek compete tent medical and legal advice as noted throughout this book. The author accepts no liability for individual outcomes.

All rights reserved. No part of this book may be reproduced without written permission from the publisher or copyright holder, except in the case of brief quotations for articles and/or reviews.

Copyright 1998
Gloria Edmonson-Nelson
1st. Revision 2001
2nd. Revision 2011
ISBN: 0-9668232-3-0

Glo's Prose Publishers
P. O. Box 45770
Los Angeles, CA. 90045
Email: GEdmon1800@aol.com
Website: Glospros.org

Printed in the United States of America

TABLE OF CONTENTS

	Page
Part I - Types of Abuse	8
Child Abuse	10
Domestic Violence	54
Emotional Abuse	66
Part II - Causes of Abuse (Why People Violate Others)	71
Part III - How to Alleviate Abuse (The Role of Communication)	80
Part IV - Why Do People Remain in Abusive Relationships (Reasons People Stay with Abusers)	85
Part V - Healing and Recovery (Overcoming Abuse)	124
Part VI - Summary (What Can Society Do to Prevent Violence?)	137
Part VII - Reclaiming Your Birthright (Testimonies of Survivors)	152
Your Birthright Entitlements	156

Glossary	**174**
Organizations	**177**
Bibliography	**199**
About the Author	**209**

INTRODUCTION

We live in a very violent society! In fact, violence has become a way of life in America, according to R. J. Gelles and M. A. Straus, authors of Physical Violence in American Families. They believe the family is the most violent institution other than the military in time of war! That is appalling, as children are also practicing this behavior. When children as young as three years of age are shooting their brothers and sisters; we have problems! Are they coming from the wombs angry? We must break the cycles of abuse!

In order to save our children and future generations, the violence must be stopped! To do this, we have to stop violating them as well as to prevent them from seeing it. According to Gelles and Straus (who will be referred to as G&S) who interviewed over 6,000 American families, 50% of the men reported they frequently assaulted their wives and children. This is overwhelming because the word "frequently" is used, and there are no statistics on those who were physically violent on one occasion, and it does not reveal the numbers who were emotionally or sexually abusive, so the statistics are even greater!

My initial premise was to write a book on child abuse because I am constantly reminded on a daily basis of the abuses rendered to infants, children, and teens. More importantly, I am sickened each time I hear the reports of children being sexually abused. What kind of "animal" would desire sex with an infant or child, and what type of person would kill an innocent, helpless person? These questions lead me to write this book.

When I began collecting information, I did not plan to discuss my past experiences with emotional and physical violence, however, as the project evolved, it was necessary to include other types of abuse. Because I am a survivor of domestic violence (I do not use the word "victim" because I am healed) by two husbands, the book includes many of my past experiences as well as those of my three sons. Although I have overcome these atrocities, I must admit that it still bothers me when I hear or see another individual being victimized, especially helpless individuals, and anyone who does not recognize that they are being violated. Other than physical violence, sometimes the abuse is not easy to delineate; in fact, it also took many years for me to understand the various types because I did not grow up in a violent household.

Who are the abusers? Most people believe males are the perpetrators. Before we move on, we must first clarify that they are not; females are also abusers! Some women violate children and their partners just as men do. In fact, "abuse by females is on the rise," according to Mel Feit, Founder and Executive Director of the National Center for Men, Old Bethpage, N.Y., one of the first male organizations to deal with violence. While doing the research on child abuse, I overhead Feit on <u>The Maury Povich Show </u>(January 22, 1997) discussing the issue of male abuse. I was alarmed to hear him say that female-to-male violence was about 50-50, and female abusers (if reported) might even be higher! My first reaction was to disagree; however, I believed that further research was required in the area of male as victim in order to understand the causes of child abuse.

I contacted Feit and was shocked to learn

some of the gory details, as well as to hear that many people, even with his factual data, disagreed with him, especially some of the feminist groups and the media. (See section on Male Abuse in my book entitled, <u>Recognizing Abuse: Reclaiming Your Birthright</u>.) Whether there is consensus or not regarding Feit's theory, we must admit that America has serious problems, and whether it is male or female as dominant abuser, the truth must be told, the issues addressed, and preventative measures sought in order to stop the atrocities. I agree with Geraldo (attorney, reporter, and famous talk show host) when he says, "Violence is violence; whether it is man, woman, or child; we must alleviate it!"

There are many differences of opinion as to what is considered abusive or violent, especially those working in the area of child abuse. For example, many child psychologists, social workers, and researchers have differences of opinions as to the meaning of sexual abuse. This is reiterated in the report "Child Abuse, Statistics, Research, Resources," by Jim Hooper, Ph.D. He believes there will always be a disagreement because child abuse and neglect are controversial. Some researchers and therapist, according to Hooper, consider "flashing" or exposing oneself to a child under age 16 as sexual abuse, while others disagree. Some experts report touching or coercion as a violation, while others use age and gender as the determining factors. For example, if an older female has sex with a boy 14 years of age and over, many do not include this as sexual abusive, and some people will take the age of the offender into consideration to determine whether the act was abusive.

To determine the numbers of children being abused; authors, experts, and therapists' biases have to be considered. Hopper provides an honest assessment when he says most experts who claim to be unbiased are fooling themselves and admits his values, intellect, and experiences as a therapist have influenced his findings. I abhor the notion of anyone using their powers or force to take advantage of another human being, especially children and the elderly who are helpless, so my biases also have to be taken into consideration! For example, I do not agree with those who use gender as the dominant factor. If a 14-year old has sex with a four-year old, or a 30-year old has sex with a 14-year old (no matter what the gender) both of these cases should be considered as rape or sexual abuse!

    The other differences in statistical information, which you will read from report-to-report, is the type of methodology used to collect information. It is Hooper's opinion that researchers should not use the word "abuse" in order to obtain information; instead, they should use behavioral descriptions rather than definitions. He says if you ask someone whether they drank more than six alcoholic drinks in one sitting, the respondent might answer "yes," but if you ask whether he/she is an alcoholic, the response would probably be "no."

    Although 90% of my respondents returned the anonymous questionnaire, I did use the word "abuse" to obtain the results. Several respondents, however, mailed them back without answering the questions, responding they could not complete it because their issues "resurfaced," and it was too painful for them to complete.

    Another variable to be considered is the difference in processes used to collect data. Hooper says face-to-face interviews might bring a different response than telephone or written because people are embarrassed to tell the truth. For example, a man might not report that he had unwanted sex with another man (even if it was forced) if he is in person, however, he might share this in written form. I believe my statistics are quite accurate because of this.

Some people ask "gate" questions (where respondents are asked a series of questions about possible abusive experiences in order to obtain a "yes" or "no" answer) which is the type of questionnaire I used. If this procedure is used, and the response is negative, questioning is discontinued. If the answer is "yes," further questions are asked. It is Hooper's belief that this procedure might, in fact, slant the results. For example, if you are trying to determine if a person was sexually abused before a certain age, and you ask; "Were you abused before age 16?" The respondent might answer "no," and that would probably terminate the interview, however, if you rephrase the question to: "Before age 16, did anyone fondle you or use threats to force you to have sex?" By framing your question in this manner, you might obtain a different answer. Another example is, "Did you feel uncomfortable around any family member because of his/her touching or using dirty or derogatory language?" That same person who initially answered "no" might respond with "yes."

For the above reasons, it is very difficult to know exactly how many people have been sexually violated due to their understanding, clarity of the question, memory, etc., however, most researchers believe there are many more than reported. For the above-mentioned reasons, many theorists' reports are lower regarding male abuse, while others are slightly higher. You can also understand why so many people disagree with Feit's conclusions. (Even though he has interviewed hundreds of adult males.) It is also the reason there is so much controversy regarding the statistics on child abuse, domestic violence, and rape.

According to Hooper, no matter how much research is conducted and by whom, the media still believes the researchers are "making up" the enormity of sexual abuse of children. He says although the majority of researchers and others will continue to disagree on the definition of abuse, at least they have become more sensitive to the need for clearly defining child sexual abuse, however, this has not been the case for commentators and critics. In other words, the whole truth about child abuse will never be accurately revealed! Because of these differences, there will always be a dichotomy; however, we should not allow these differences to keep us from working toward the common goal of preventing violence.

You will note that many of my citations are in the states of Kansas and California. I grew up in the Midwest, where I resided until age 21, later moving to California. Although they are two very different states (Kansas is considered "Bible-belt," while California is supposed to be "liberal-minded"). You will notice that violations discussed in Kansas are just as traumatic as in California, which proves parenting, material values, good schools, etc., have not made a drastic difference in reducing violence!

My goals are to educate those living in abusive situations, to inform society of the seriousness of this issue, and to evoke the emotions of adults so that we start building stronger families and making safer environments for children and youth. There are many other people working toward these same goals. Frank Sinatra, famous singer and "icon" who died in 1988 reportedly left 150 million dollars in his Will for the purpose of building a center for abused children in California! Another famous actress, Carol Channing, recently spoke out after 31 years of emotional, physical, and sexual abuse. It was very sad to hear an elderly woman explain how her husband and manager allegedly used his powers to control her. (He is alleged to have controlled all monetary affairs, and she never saw her paycheck the 31 years she was married, and reported he only slept with her on two occasions!) When she appeared on Barbara Walters, <u>The View</u>, (May 22, 1998) I could feel her pain when she said she felt betrayed. When asked why she waited so long to come forth, she responded, "I was not aware, but now I am. I want to help other women grab the ball and run with it!" She said she wanted to help young women to recognize abuse earlier than she did. She is to be commended for her honesty because most victims who live to be her age usually die without every receiving their healing. This book was finally completed after many revisions coupled with anger, inspiration, sleepless nights, coffee, but most of all, as a result of lots of prayers!

PART I
RECOGNIZING ABUSE

TYPES OF ABUSE

Thirty-five years ago I was a victim of domestic violence, and although I physically removed myself from the situation, it took many years for me to understand that I had been emotionally abused several years prior to the actual physical incident. Had I recognized the signals ("red flags") it would not have taken five years to leave! There are many people who are not aware they are being violated because they are addicted, codependent, in denial, or living in fear. Whatever the reasoning, no one should be victimized!

As stated previously, there are many definitions of "abuse," but <u>Webster's New World Dictionary</u> (1968) defines it as: "to make wrong use of, to ill treat, violate, revile, malign, or improper treatment." Roget's International Thesaurus defines abuse in the noun tense as: "berating, curse, mistreatment, misuse, and ravishment." In the verb tense, the uses are: "berate, blaspheme, curse, misuse, ravish, use badly, and work evil." If any of these words describe how your are being treated by another person; you are definitely being abused, and you could possibly become a death statistic!
If you are not a victim, you could be an abuser and not be aware. Then, there are those who are both victim and perpetrator! If you believe you can be classified in any of the above categories, this book can help you to "reclaim your birthright powers" which will lead you to peace and freedom!

I was fortunate to grow up in a stable family where love, not abuse, was the base. For people who have not had this good fortune, according to G&S, it is a long battle because some people repeat the denial and self-destructive behavior that they received. When children do not have permanent, positive relationships with adults (extended or otherwise) and are unable to trace positive roots, sometimes they are unable to become competent and stable adults. For example, some children go from foster home-to-foster home, never being able to get close to anyone! The majority will only stay there long enough to get adjusted and are then removed, placed in another temporary one, and in many cases, back into the hands of Child Protective Services or adoption agencies. If these children do not have counseling, many become society's problems through no fault of their own!

Although it has been a decade since G&S's theory, and many people are working toward rebuilding the family structure, my research does not reveal any drastic changes in this area. In fact, divorce rates have increased. It is reported that one out of every two marriages will end in divorce, or we can assume that the divorce rate is approximately 50%. It is imperative that we continually search for peace for the children and others who are in crisis situations!

If you are not being physically abused, you might be the victim of emotional violence by your mate, family members, friends, or employer. Sometimes we miss the initial signals or prefer to conveniently ignore them because of the following reasons: sexual, financial, or an emotional involvement, fear of being alone, children, materialism, etc. Sometimes we believe the abuser will change, and some do, but many psychotherapists and other child abuse experts believe some people never change. For example, many pedophiles are reported to be unable to be around children unless they violate or have the desire.

Many of the television talk show hosts have done an excellent job in educating in the area of child abuse: Oprah Winfrey, Maury Povich, Leeza Gibbons, Geraldo, and the first one, Phil Donahue, to name a few. They are helping to bring many issues of violence to the forefront, when, in the past, there were really no "vehicles" in which to share this information. Because of these shows, many males, females, teens, and children are now coming forth to discuss their pains. Prior to these shows, many people lived with their pains because so they were either too embarrassed or fearful that they would not be believed, a family member or role model would be exposed, or they did not realize they were being violated. Because many women are now realizing through these shows that they have choices, many are returning to work, school, etc., which gives them more independence and resources to leave. In some relationships, this change has caused more problems because the abuser believes he has lost control. In some cases, her success has created a different set of problems. For the male victim, through these shows and other organizations, he also realizes that he has rights, such as joint custody of children, receiving a portion of the wife's retirement, and half of the assets. In previous years, this was unknown.

CHILD ABUSE:

"It takes a village to raise a child" is an old

adage now being used by our politicians. In fact, in 1998, Hillary Rodham Clinton (then First Lady - now Senator) sent letters to Democratic voters that read, "Children's issues are bigger than politics." I agree with her totally! Although your approach to this issue might be quite different from Mrs. Clinton's or mine, you have no choice but to get involved when it comes to child abuse. It is not enough to say that you are not qualified, uneducated, untrained, or that you do not have time or money. One of your family members could possibly be the next victim of physical or sexual abuse, incest, or maybe the abuser! Preserving the future generations is society's role. Whether you desire to get involved or not, most of the murderers, rapists, or incarcerated pedophiles use the jail and prison system as a "revolving" door, so we are all supporting them by paying taxes!

In 1998, Maury Povich featured a show on child abuse. The psychologist gave a grizzly report: five children are killed per day from abuse: more than the number killed in car accidents! Another NBC Report on Child Abuse, February 6, 1997, revealed children are 12 times more likely to die by gunfire in the United States than any other country, and the most depressing part of child abuse is that many are violated by role models or "acquaintance abuse."

As drastic as the statistics might sound G&S did not find that all abused children grow up to become abusers; in other words, they are not preprogrammed. They did find that some children who were abused tend to grow up to be abusive. In fact, they cited a case of one male at a lecture who said he stayed single because he was afraid he would abuse his own children! Another teen male was alleged to have killed an 11-year old boy months after being sexually molested by an adult male. (The Oakland Tribune, November 13, 1999.)

Surprisingly, according to G&S, most abused children or incest victims love their parents and are "tied" to their abusers by the love and affection. For example, an associate writer, after learning of my writing this book, called me to share her experience. She related how she was thrown over an overpass in New York by her alcoholic mother at about the age of two weeks and was found on the train tracks. She said she only recalls being hospitalized at age seven for a spine operation. Of interest is that she has no bad feelings against her mother, and said she understands her mother did what she did because she had six children that she could not feed!

Anyone can be found guilty of child abuse, so do not immediately discount a child's allegations because the accused is someone you know, a role model, family member, or elderly man or woman. I am sad to report that people from each of those groups have been found guilty of sexual abuse. Anyone who is able to come in close contact with children is able to violate. For example, a 61-year old male teacher who had taught at public and parochial schools was found guilty of molesting girls over a 30-year period. After being on probation, he was recently charged with downloading pornographic pictures of children from the Internet. He was held on one million dollars bail while awaiting arraignment. (Los Angeles Times, March 24, 2000.)

Another very violent case of child abuse involved two brothers who were found chained to their bedposts by dog chains! It was not a stranger who performed this act; it was their mother, father, and aunt! The two boys ages 17 and 12 were filthy, underdeveloped, in poor health as well as signs of physical and emotional neglect. It is alleged that signs on the fence and walls read: "God's country," "Spirit of God," etc. (<u>Los Angeles Sentinel</u>, October 19-25, 2000.)

There are no statistics on the oldest, but an 80-year old grandfather was convicted in August 2000 of molesting two neighbor girls ages 12 and 14. He was accused six years prior of molesting his two granddaughters who tried to kill him (the gun did not go off), but they had to serve six months! They said they had tried for years to get people to believe them, but no one did. Because of their testimony, and that of another granddaughter, he was finally convicted of 10 years in prison for the recent case! (<u>WAVE</u> Newspaper, August 23, 2000.)

Another case of overwhelming forgiveness by a victim (which most people will remember because it was so traumatic) involved a father, who allegedly poured kerosene over his infant son's body because he was upset with the mother! The boy, now in his 20's, has had 35 operations. He confronted his father on television to let him know that he had been forgiven. The young man is now a movie producer, has a girlfriend, and although still disfigured, he is happy because he is not holding a grudge and has gone on to empower himself. When he was talking to his father, you could feel that he truly loved him and was not blaming him. This confirms G&S's theory that children still love their abusers, no matter what is rendered to them!

Some of you will be surprised to know that when one child is physically or sexually abused and the other is not but is aware, there is jealousy on the part of the one who is not! G&S share that many children suffer as if they were being victimized. It is their theory that because children learn early in life that those who love you are those who hit you, they believe it is morally okay. The authors found similar findings in victims of incest or sexual abuse, who believe they are loved if they are abused! Another theory as to why children are affected is that they are unable to help the victim; however, this rationale usually relates to older children. In fact, some people are not abused will suffer even more, because they blame themselves for being unable to stop the abuse!

You would think that parents would never violate a disabled child, but there are those who have abused children for years. For example, a father and stepmother in Northern California were alleged to have abused a boy with Down syndrome for many years. He had been removed from the home and living in a foster home for several years. The parents were put on five year's probation and received counseling, however, Child Protective Services said they investigated and found no problems. After he was returned to the family (against the foster parent's advice) he was again emotionally and physically violated again, this time by the stepmother. The foster mother said she had told them the boy would be abused again, but nobody believed her. The attorney, representing the father, said he was a good Christian. His main concern was the father would have to go to jail on the holiest day of the year..." The cases were to be handled separately; hopefully someone will be held accountable, and the boy will be permanently removed from their care.

In the recent years, there have been many

reports of beating deaths by young parents. In one case a 15-year old girl allegedly beat her 9-month-old son who died of brain trauma. Her boyfriend was also arrested for unlawful sexual intercourse with a minor (the mother). In another case a 25-year old man allegedly sexually molested his three-month old daughter! The child died from multiple head injuries, including a fractured skull. (<u>Los Angeles Times</u>, May 24, 2000.) Whatever the reasoning, society must help young parents understand that abuse is not the answer to their stresses. People with knowledge should report suspicious behavior of child abuse to Child Protective Services or their local police departments.

<u>Signals of Sexual Abuse in Children</u>. Most children do not, or cannot, tell anyone that they are being sexually abused; so it is up to parents or concerned adults to recognize the signs. According to the Sexual Assault Crisis Center of Knoxville, Tennessee (5/21/97) it is difficult to tell if a child has been sexually molested unless there is evidence of physical or behavioral signals. The problem with this is that there is no single behavior that definitely determines whether a child has been sexually violated. The general behavior changes that may occur in children are:

- physical complaints
- fear or dislike of certain people or places
- headaches
- sleep disturbances
- school problems
- excessive bathing or poor hygiene
- discipline problems

- anxiety
- depression
- low self-esteem
- hostility or aggression
- sexual activity, pregnancy at early age
- withdrawal from family, friends, or usual activities, and suicide attempts.

These are just a few of the behavior problems; however, children who have been sexually abused repeatedly have more specific symptoms as follows:

- paining or swelling, bleeding or irritation of the mouth, genital, or anal areas,
- talking about the abuse indirectly
- having bladder infections or sexually-transmitted diseases
- act out sexual behavior.

Then there is the silent problem with children who do not tell anyone about their sexual abuse because they:

- are too young
- Were threatened or bribed
- feel confused by the abuser's attention
- are afraid no one will believe them
- blame themselves
- believe punishment is for being "bad"
- get themselves and others in trouble.

Silence, however, enables the abuse to continue because it protects the offenders and hurts the children. There are so many resources available now; children no longer have to suffer in silence. As adults, we have a responsibility to protect children. In fact, one of their "birthright entitlements" is to feel safe.

Many children and adults are aware of abuse but afraid to report it for many reasons; they believe other family members will alienate them. For example, one of the interviewees reported her 30-year old brother to authorities after her five-year old niece (his daughter) told her what he had done. It was later learned that he had been sexually molesting the child allegedly during her infant years. The wife was reportedly very fearful of him, so if she knew, did not report it. When the aunt reported it, instead of the family supporting her in this effort, some of them alienated her for many years because he was incarcerated. He was later released after going through counseling. The victim, who is now grown with two children of her own, has reunited with her father and mother. Both the mother and victim have forgiven him, and are grateful that the aunt reported him.

Some brave children do, however, report their parents and others and are not afraid because they know sexual abuse is wrong! For example, in Southern California, a young girl packing to go on vacation with her family found a videotape of her 50-year old father with children performing oral sex on him. It was later learned there was a total of 75 videotapes involving four children, and he had paid a woman $200 per child to find the children, and also paid their parents! He received a sentence of 32 felony counts. Although the girl is to be commended, she will probably require therapy to understand and overcome what she saw.

There are other types of violations that are

more controversial. You might remember the 13-year old Berkeley, California, girl who weighed 680 lbs., who was found dead after allegedly being found in urine with bedsores. It was reported the mother believed she was a good parent, but just could not take care of her. The judge said it was the conditions in which the child was found that initially sent her to jail. Many people supported the mother, stating she had no choice because the girl was just too large for her to care for. Most people supported this women stating she had no choice because the girl was too large for her to care for and believe that probation is the proper sentence. Many helpless parents are in similar conditions as this mother was. Should you or someone you know become helpless, do not allow negligence, finances, or depressed conditions cause you to be the abuser - the rules are changing, and you will go to jail!

  There are many situations similar to the above which are abusive to children, but they are questionable as to whether the parent(s) are responsible or not. In some cases the children are removed from the household by Child Protective Services even when the parent(s) have no direct knowledge. For example, when a relative abuses a child, and the parents are not aware; they are charged. Even though you cannot always be with your children, CPS and others will hold you responsible. You must, therefore, teach them how to also recognize the signals of abuse, as well as how to cope, and how to be safe at every stage of development. You must inform your children how to protect themselves from sexual abuse, just as you would teach them to avoid fires, water, and other health-related precautions. For example, teach them:

- they are loved and valued, and they deserve to be safe (as my mother did)
- their body belongs to them, and no one should touch them inappropriately
- the differences between safe and unsafe touches
- the proper names for all body parts, so they will be able to communicate them clearly should they have to report abuse. As soon as they can talk, use the words vagina, penis, rectum, etc., so they can describe to you exactly what happened. (Do not use slang words like many parents do because they will not be understood).
- that safety rules apply to all adults, even family members, role models, family friends, and not just strangers
- that some adults have problems
- they can say "no" to requests that make them feel uncomfortable—even from a close relative, family friend, or anyone else.
- to report if any adult asks them to keep a secret. Make sure they know that you will believe and protect them if they tell you about an abusive act.
- to tell a trusted adult about abuse, even if they are afraid because they have been threatened. (Some abusive family members or friends will tell the child they will kill themselves, the child, the mother, or parents).

The last one should be emphasized with the child because some children might believe that because the parents, mother, or foster parent are not available, they should not tell anyone else. For example, at school, children should be instructed to tell the teacher (if he/she is the abuser, another teacher should be told), the counselor, school psychologist, or the principal.

Adults, caretakers, etc. should also practice listening to children because many do not until it is too late. There are effective ways to listen so that you can determine if he/she has been violated. They are as follows:

- Keep calm - The children should know that you are not angry, however, they can interpret anger or disgust as being directed towards them. This should be reiterated.
- Believe the child - According to the Crisis Center, most children do not lie about sexual abuse.
- Give positive messages and tell them they are not to blame.
- Respect the child's privacy.
- Do not panic or overreact when the child talks about the experience. They need your help and support.
- Do not pressure the child to talk or avoid talking about the abuse. Allow the child to talk at his/her own pace. Forcing information can be harmful, and sometimes children believe they must say something, and a few have been known to create additional untrue facts.

Do not confront the offender in the child's presence. It might be too harmful. Leave this job to the authorities.

- Be responsible by reporting the incident to the Department of Human Services. Most states have laws indicating that reporting abuse does not mean that it has only means that you have seen indicators of abuse or have reason to suspect. Understand that there will, in fact, be an investigation, and in most cases, the truth will be revealed, even in the few cases where a child does lie.

- Arrange a medial exam. Get professional counseling, even if it is only for a short time.

If abuse is cycled from generation-to-generation, it is hard to stop, says Gary Sprague, author of "Breaking the Cycle." He says we need to educate our children about abuse, and what they can do to stop it. Kids should know that if their safety is in danger, they must tell someone so they can be protected, and the abuser can get professional help.

Pedophile Abuse. Gavin de Becker, author of Protecting the Gift, expert on child abuse and other issues, has reported that for every square mile in America, there is a sexual molester! He stresses the importance of using one's intuition and not denying those intuitions as to who will violate, that we should not wait until a crime is committed to confirm those suspicions. In other words, we should not "wait for the part of the puzzle that confirms those suspicions." He provides valuable advice in order to protect children and adults as follows:

- Do not volunteer children to help a stranger to look for a dog in the park
- Do not help strangers carry packages to their car.

Conversely, de Becker says it is wrong to tell children not to talk to strangers because they will violate them. Most parents do not understand that most of the abusers are family members or associates! He shared a story about a woman who teaches her seven-year old son to go up and talk with strangers, so that he has an ability to recognize a potential abuser, when another child would not be able to.

From his years of research, de Becker has found that children who talk to strangers are less likely to be abused! I must admit, I was shocked to hear this theory because we were also taught as children to "watch out for strangers." Another fact that de Becker stresses is that parents should not make children kiss adults - even relatives. When children do not feel good about a person, they should not have to hug or kiss them. It is his opinion that children are given "God-given" intuitions, as well as mothers, and we should not be afraid to use them. He says parents are in "signals of denial," that they must be willing to believe that people close to the family are the molesters; however, most people are not! He says people will ask what the signals are of a potential family or associate who would violate. It is his opinion that the warning signs are inside the mother - her intuition! Whether you agree with de Becker or not, one cannot be too cautious when parenting young children.

Is There Hope for Pedophiles? Many psychiatrists, psychologists, and others working in the area of child abuse, believe pedophiles (men who molest children) are never healed, however, there are differences of opinion. Some people believe that most pedophiles are created because they are abused children who were never healed. Others are of the opinion that they violate because they have mental/emotional problems, for example, brain damage at birth, etc. Because each case varies, it is difficult to know whether therapy, alone, is a cure-all. Many pedophiles have stated they have certain feelings around children, and these feelings do not occur when they are in the company of adults.

One pedophile admitted that even with punishment, therapy, etc., that the feelings still "erupt like a volcano again" until the act is repeated on someone else! For example, a 62-year old male reported he could not go around his sister's young sons and daughters on holidays because of these feelings. He explained that he never received help until a male teen reported his acts to the boss at the fast food job. Because he offered the 14-year old money in exchange for sex on more than one occasion, the boy, who refused, was able to prosecute. The family was not aware that he was a pedophile because he never told them. He said on one occasion the feelings were so strong toward his niece and nephew, he knew he was not completely healed. Not only did he join a group, but he also joined a church. This man was victimized fourteen years by an uncle who lived with his family, he said he now understands that his problem has to be nurtured at all times. He likens it to an alcoholic around alcohol, stating something has to replace it. He is in a 12-step program and following the teachings of metaphysics. (A spiritual philosophy which deals with cause and effect and the power of positive thinking.) His story was one of the most touching. This man has learned that he has to take one day at a time. The most important factor is that he understands that in order to be whole, he has to "face his demons" and take responsibility for his actions.

One psychologist, who wrote to Landers about sexual abuse of children, said pedophiles should be offered counseling, and it should take place during prison sentences. She opines that sentences should never be reduced for good behavior and does not believe these abusers are cured, even with therapy, and they should not be given the opportunity to find new victims! Although I do not have factual information regarding the percentage of male sexual offenders who repeat the acts, I agree with her recommendation that counseling should be given during incarceration.

Vermont has incorporated a similar program that has been in practice since 1983. According to the Director of Correctional Services, it is highly effective. Although some people might not agree with their procedure, fewer than 6 percent committed the same crimes in the seven years following release! (As reported by Alan Elsner, February 22, 2001, AOL). For offenders who did not receive or complete the treatment, the return rate was 30 percent! Apparently it has been very successful. The therapy is called "masturbatory reconditioning" and is taught by a therapist. Pedophiles have to develop adult sexual fantasies, followed by masturbation in private to those fantasies. According to Therapist Gary Allen, the fantasies must be age appropriate, in the context of a relationship, consensual, respectful, and mutually satisfying. After orgasm, they have to stimulate themselves for another 30 minutes while reverting to their deviant fantasies. They are required to use words including the victim's age and acknowledge the fact that it is by force. The aim, according to Allen, is to create boredom in order to get rid of the deviant fantasy. The sessions are recorded on an audiotape that the therapist reviews to make sure the inmates are carrying out the technique correctly. The treatment is repeated at least 20 times!

Another part of the therapy includes victims coming to prison to speak with offenders who have to role-play as if they were the victims. They also imagine their are committing an offense, but it is interrupted by sniffing ammonia in order to break the sexual build-up. They have to imagine they are being caught in the act.

The final therapeutic method is where inmates are attached to a machine where a computer charts their arousal while slides are flashed in front of them. This helps therapists monitor what causes the prisoner to become aroused to assess the degree of normal versus deviant arousal. Following release, offenders have to attend group therapy once a week for two to three years. Although some people might find the above-mentioned healing processes as too stringent, but they are working. For example, one offender, age 54, who went through the program after assaulting his 13-year old stepdaughter, said the effect on him was immense. He said "It was very hard and scary to look at myself honestly and face up to what I had did. I used to feel sorry for myself all the time. I didn't care about others," he said. He said he was changed sexually and his thought processes are now changed. He has now remarried, said he was honest with his wife has been honest with his wife, and has been out for four years!

Some states have incorporated parts of this procedure into their program and others have passed legislation for "chemical castration" where offenders are injected with a hormone to reduce testosterone levels in order to receive parole.

According to the report, once the medication is stopped, the person soon becomes a threat again. Because of this, and other factors previously discussed, most sex therapists, psychologists, and others working on behalf of children, believe pedophiles should either be incarcerated or placed in separate housing away from children.

Some sex offenders are now seeking castration in order to be dismissed from prison. In the report "Some Sex Offenders Seek Controversial Procedure," Los Angeles Times, (March 2, 2001) although some of the prisoners have been in and out of prison for years. In fact, one 62-year old man had spent half of his life behind bars, and most of his convictions were for molestation of boys younger than 15 years old! (One was nine years old). He served six years for those crimes, was released, and within two years he had committed other sex offenses! He served another ten years, but the judge believed he would probably victimize again and committed him indefinitely. He is now requesting voluntary castration in order to be released. Thus far, two judges have denied his requests, but he has appealed stating his sexual appetites have waned as he has grown older and that being castrated would fully curb them."

Another man was granted his request for castration in 1997 after being convicted three times in 14 years for fondling young boys. He was sent to a mental hospital. After fearing lifetime commitment, he requested castration. Because the judge said he believed the man was sincere, that the operation would help him. After the operation, he was released but has to register as a sex offender and report frequently. To this date, it appears as if he has not violated another person. According to the article, he believes that he has been permanently cured; that he sees kids near the hotel where he lives, but he does not pay them any attention. He went on to say, "It does not faze me like it used to. I used to think bad things."

Many prosecutors and others who are opposed to freeing men argue that the operation does not always eliminate deviate sexual urges, that they should still be closely monitored. Others argue that hormones are also produced by other glands, because the amounts vary from man to man, it is difficult to predict who will commit more crimes. Others contest because they say pedophiles can simply buy hormone replacement medications from a pharmacy. Still others say there are other pedophiles whose fantasies stem from mental not physical, and the most violent sex offenders are not affected by castration because their behavior is more psychologically than physically based.

Whether to castrate and release sexual offenders remains a very difficult decision. With taxpayers paying $107,000 for each one housed in a state mental hospital, versus allowing the surgery, or requiring it, is a "touchy" situation. One never knows whether the person will violate or kill another child. For example, the defender who helped the above person obtain the castration said he initially opposed it but changed his mind after learning about the long history. He believes others are now inspired to do the same thing and this "troubles" him. He also considers the surgery barbaric, according to this article. Proponents, however, say castration is a humane treatment for people seeking to rid themselves of a largely incurable, dangerous, sexual disorder!

Effects of Child Abuse. Even those children who are emotionally abused suffer from a number of problems which make them difficult to raise, says G&S. They share the case of a couple who adopted a four-year old who had been burned on his back with cigarettes. During the first eight years he was quiet and withdrawn, but as he became a teen-ager he began responding to the couple by using obscenities if they challenged him, as well as using drugs, skipping school, and threatening the wife with her husband's gun!

    The authors admit that they have limited knowledge about long-term effects of abuse rendered during early years, and my research, as well as that of others, has proven the same. There were no reports to determine whether abused infants suffered any more than abused children or teens. In fact, G&S (who are well-respected experts in the area of child abuse) were unable to find anyone who had investigated abused infants through adolescence and on into adult life. They were only able to learn effects of abuse from older children and adults who retrospectively shared past abuse and present situations. Most of the respondents of my study remembered being abused at about age 12 (boys and girls) and other than physical beatings, they were unable to recall sexual abuse. As stated previously, many children "block out" the abuse in order to survive. In fact, research has revealed that only one out of three adults can remember being sexually abused as a child. Research results, however, does show that children who grow up in violent homes have lower test scores, exhibit learning problems, and many have to attend special classes. One common personality trait all children from violent homes exhibit is aggressiveness and defensiveness.

Some children will draw themselves without arms or hands, and many abused children go on to become juvenile delinquents. Conversely, there are some who survive unhappy childhood, and again, researchers have only been able to surmise that some nurturing person (grandparent, relative, foster parent, or other role model) was responsible in helping a child overcome the abuse.

Effects of Sexual Abuse. According to Karen Davis, President of the Commonwealth Fund, as quoted in the article "Abused Teen Girls Likely to Face Host of Other Troubles," sexual abuse puts the victim on a dangerous path. This is confirmed in three private studies as follows:

- In the state of Washington they were more than twice as likely to have had sexual intercourse and three times as likely to get pregnant.
- In a Midwestern state, teen-agers with a history of sexual abuse were likely to have more sexual partners than other teen-agers.
- In the Commonwealth survey, girls who had been sexually or physically abused were more likely to be depressed, smoke, drink alcohol, and use drugs.

Dr. Jacqueline Stock, researcher who conducted the Washington study, states when sexual experiences are coercive, demeaning, and too early, it can make girls feel that their primary worth is related to sexuality, and they are more likely to consider suicide. It is Davis' opinion that information should be a "wake-up" call to everyone.

Hooper, quoted previously, cites from the

research of Linda Williams entitled, "Recovered Memories of Sexual Abuse: Scientific Research & Scholarly Resources," where she reports at least 10% of people sexually abused in childhood will have periods of complete amnesia of their abuse, followed by experiences of delayed recall. Some experts, however, dispute this theory. He says it is not rare for victims to say they don't remember being abused, or that there were times they did not remember an act of abuse that they now remember.

Abuse victims are affected in many ways, and some are abused for so many years that they develop ways to deal with it through repression or dissociation, however, it is never totally forgotten. In fact, many victims recall it in dreams, nightmares, flashbacks, and behavioral reenactments, and some people suffer from post-traumatic stress syndrome after being abused. This condition usually develops following a severe action, which many victims cannot forget, however, there are some who live with it after one violation. Many of the veterans suffer from this illness following war, and it has caused many to be on drugs, homeless, and on medication or disability for the rest of their lives! It exhibits itself in panic attacks, anxiety, nightmares, paranoia, and flashbacks, and some veterans have reported that the memories will always be with them. This inability to cope with the severity of repeated sexual violations has caused some children this same permanent damage, as if they had fought in a war!

Because of the pain, some children develop ways to "hide" the abuse; consequently, some of the facts might be missing. It is sometimes difficult for the victims, who in many cases, is dependent on the abuser, consequently they learn to partially block the abuse. Amnesia, then, enables the victim to maintain an attachment with the abuser, especially if that person is a vital person in the victim's life. According to Judith Lewis Herman, M.D., who has done extensive research in this area, evidence shows that these children suffer the most devastating psychological trauma. Some of these children grow up with the inability to develop and maintain intimate relationships with other people, due to the inability to trust anyone. Even with therapy, it has been reported that the pains are too deeply embedded.

In most occasions, the effects to the child are greater than the punishment to the abuser or pedophile. For example, in New Jersey in 1999, a man who molested a teen months before the teen killed an 11-year old neighbor, received only five years in prison. Not only that, it is said that he could be eligible for parole in four months based on the two years he has already served! This is horrible - this boy was not only violated, will live with those pains for years; but he will also be punished for reacting apparently to what happened to him. We must change the laws to make certain the punishment fits the crime! Even if he had served two years - we must make stricter laws because this abuser can be released in four months to possibly molest another child!

Cyberspace Sexual Abuse. A new type of pedophile abuse occurred in 1996 at the birth of the computer's Internet. Although this viable tool has been very helpful to educate as well as bring information and people together, it has caused some parents grief because they have not monitored their children and teens' activities. Since its inception, there have been many complaints of sexual abuse and/or pornography of children through the computer, and many people have been caught. For example, in California several males were caught luring boys to other states for sexual purposes. They allegedly represented themselves as another child or teen.

    Another 47-year old male was sentenced to four years, nine months in prison for asking a 14-year old girl to send him sexually-explicit photographs of herself, as reported in the August, 1997 <u>Parsons Sun Newspaper</u>. Prosecutors said he allegedly met her in the chat room when she was 12 years of age, posing as a 15-year old boy. Although the girl never physically met with the man, she is reported to have written a letter stating her life was destroyed because she felt emotionally raped. This man is supposed to have had relationships with at least five other girls. He pled guilty to inducing a minor to produce child pornography. As a result, this judge requested that parents around the nation monitor their children's computer use.

    Another woman reported her husband would go to a chat room on the <u>Internet</u>, and she caught him asking for pictures of little girls being sexually molested. The woman said she cried all evening because he had already downloaded several pictures, and she begged him to get help because they had five small grandchildren. The husband allegedly said he did not have a problem. She was writing to ask "Dear Abby" whether the husband could also be a child molester because he sent out a picture of his own daughter! According to the article, the advice was to report him to the police immediately! (<u>Los Angeles Times</u>, December 11, 2000.)

There are many cases similar to the one cited above, in fact, because it has become so rampant, many internet providers have added "watch-dog" type policing systems in an attempt to catch abusers. Some providers have placed adults in the chat room to pose as a child in order to catch adults. It is proving to be very beneficial; one boy was supposed to meet a man in San Francisco, but the police met him instead! There are, however, many others who are luring children and teens because parents do not monitor them.

Sometimes the abuser will lure children or teens away by promising various monetary or other attractive items. In California a six-year old female child who was using the computer unsupervised, was told to come outside of her home. The male told her that he would bring candy, but she should not tell anyone. This youngster was smart enough to tell her mother, but apparently the man became suspicious, did not appear, and was never caught. Hopefully he will be arrested so that another child will not become his prey!

Because of the national concern regarding cyberspace child abuse and pornography, America Online and other service providers have developed controls on the computer in an attempt to prevent abuse. For example, <u>AOL</u> has installed a system called "mail control." Through this device parents can insert certain information or codes to prevent unwanted users. Even with this device, cyberspace abuse continues. <u>AOL</u> has also added a reporting or referring system for unwanted E-mail messages. You can now send them to <u>AOL</u> for monitoring and investigation by opening the message, selecting "Forward," typing in either of the following words "TOSspam, TOSEmail1, or TosFiles as the addressee, and then send to AOL who will follow up. Hopefully this will also deter some abusers.

As authorities and judges have stated, children should not use the computer alone, and parents should have serious discussions with teens about the dangers of the chat rooms, even though many enjoy talking to boys and girls around the country. Parents should also monitor their incoming computer. For example, just recently an 11-year old shot a group of children and teachers at school. He is alleged to have been communicating with a man through the computer. The man had allegedly sexually abused the boy on several occasions. The mother stated she had assumed something was not right after reading the messages. She said she had told the man not to contact her son again, but rather than continuing to follow up, she assumed the messages had ceased when, in fact, the boy needed help. She did not learn to what extent, until after he had shot several classmates! Had his activities been consistently monitored, and the proper counseling received, maybe those students would be alive today!

I cannot say enough about the issue of policing the Internet. In September 1998, authorities reported breaking up the largest international child pornography ring in history. It is alleged that hundreds of children's pictures as young as 18-months old were being sold. These are just a few examples of how the computer's web system can be used to violate children. Because this type of abuse is running rampant, some police departments are now conducting workshops for parents to teach them how to use controls, what sites to watch for, and how to monitor chat room activity. This new type of abuse cannot be emphasized enough because people can now commit their violations while "hiding" behind this important vehicle.

More and more police departments are watching for abusers on the Internet. Sacramento's Police Department has an Investigator who sits at the computer daily for the sole purpose of catching abusers of children especially in chatrooms and pornographic sites.

How to Alleviate Child Abuse. Specialists in the field of child abuse indicate many people do not report suspicious cases because they do not have faith in Child Protective Services. Some believe they are not doing enough to save the children, for example, that there is not enough follow-through, the child sent back to the hands of the abuser, or placed in another abusive home. Others do not report suspicious cases because they either fail to recognize it, do not care to get involved, or they are afraid of interfering. One example of alleged negligence occurred at a hospital when a six-month old baby was brought to the emergency room with a lacerated vagina, and the physician is alleged to have said, "The infant has probably stuck herself!" The social worker reportedly asked the physician, "How can you view a six-month old with a lacerated vagina as a routine case?" In this case, the child abuse team was never called!

There are many other similar situations that are occurring because individuals fail to recognize a situation or complaint as abusive. I agree with G&S when they say intervention is required in order to alleviate child abuse. Hopefully this book will be a "wake-up call" to everyone, to recognize the many signals of abuse, even when they are not obvious.

I do not believe the above-cited incident is

the norm because some hospitals are now training all staff to recognize the "red flags." For example, since 1994 hospitals in Northern California are now reporting suspected cases of domestic violence to the police, however, there is no requirement for police officers to report incidents of domestic violence to Child Protective Services. Some police departments are now working with Child Protective Service Agencies and domestic violence shelters to make sure children are not abused when the mother is a victim of domestic violence, and to assure that they are not returned to the home of the abuser.

There are still some cities dealing with child abuse and domestic violence as two separate issues, consequently some children are being victimized along with the mother or father, and their abuse is never reported. In situations where a female is abused, in some cases the child has also been abused or will be. CPS should also be contacted, even if the social worker only interviews the child to determine if counseling or other help is needed. This should be implemented as routine, so there is no breakdown regarding child abuse. Phillip Babich, in his, "Spousal Abuse and Child Abuse Are Two Sides of the Same Coin," is also concerned that the various agencies: Child Protective Services, advocates for battered women, the sheriff's department, etc., are all working from different vantage points. He says there is a general belief that Alameda County's (Oakland, California and surrounding areas) system is not working well enough to protect women and children from violent husbands, boyfriends, ex-boyfriends, and fathers.

In California's San Diego County, there is a concerted effort to determine whether a child might be in danger of physical abuse, rather than waiting until they are brought to the emergency room. There is a sharing of information between all agencies. Carolyn Russel, Executive Director of "A Safe Place," a women's shelter in Alameda County, agrees that coordination between all agencies is the key, citing San Diego County's program as an exemplary one that is "far ahead," as reported by Babich.

Because so many Child Protective Service staff members are working long hours and reportedly have tremendous workloads and case files, some children have "fallen through the cracks" and are returned to the abusive situations, I believe, through no fault of theirs. Rather than blame or point fingers, we must work to assure that more social workers are hired and continued education is provided to them in order to prevent this.

Another problem, which many will debate, centers around some judges and other officials who believe it is better to keep the family together rather than punish the abuser by allowing him/her to return home. This plan works in some cases, however, there are others where the abuser is released and goes back to kill and/or molest others.

In some cases, abusers are not viewed as cruel individuals but as victims! Because of this, each community must have many shelters available to accommodate family members. Most large cities have shelters in place which are sponsored by various groups; for example, many churches are now becoming involved, and there are others funded by the State, County, United Way, and other private entities.

There are differences in opinion regarding the coordination efforts, in fact the domestic violence and child abuse cases are housed in two separate sections, and according to Lt. Hoig, Oakland Police Department (reported by Babich) child abuse is grouped with sexual assault, and domestic violence is grouped with assault. Although domestic violence doesn't always go hand in hand with child abuse, when they receive a call, they check on the kids to see if they are hurt and also inspect the condition of the house. Their primary function, however, is to separate the fighting couple, which is sometimes dangerous because upset spouses "turn on" the police.

Babich also reports some good news. Efforts are now being made to better coordinate domestic violence and child abuse in Alameda County. For example, A Safe Place has entered into an agreement with the Oakland Police Department to help with the domestic violence unit. Their staff follows up the next day and meets with the troubled family to assist with restraining orders and other legal services, if needed.

Coordinating the various agencies to work towards alleviating all violence is not an easy task, and as mentioned throughout this book, the entirety of society must be reshaped. Rita Hayes, Child Abuse Services Coordinator at Child Protective Services (cited by Babich) states categorical funding is the major barrier; and politics continues to play a role!

Role of Parents. First of all, parents should stop the violence in homes; even the arguing which is emotionally abusive to children. Dr. Phil, a frequent family counselor on The Oprah Winfrey show, states parents should say, "I'm not going to argue in front of the children." He said parents should make a lifetime decision to do this so children are not violated. Each time you holler and scream, you change the children, according to Dr. Phil, and I agree totally!

Parents, or those responsible for raising children, should monitor what a child sees on television and movies. For example, a report from the Parents Television Council (organized by Steve Allen, famous actor and activist, who died in 1999) reports television does not come close to accurately informing parents whether or not a show is suitable for their children. In other words, parents cannot trust the television rating systems regarding foul language, sexual references, and violence. They examined three weeks of network programming from 8-9 p.m. on weekdays and 7-9 p.m. on Sunday and found that 65 percent of shows that contained at least one obscenity failed to carry an "L" (offensive language), and 76 percent did not carry the "D" (suggestive dialogue) rating. The Executive Director, Mark Honig, suggests the first hour of prime-time programming should be cleaned up, however, the Motion Picture Association of America, who supervised the 14-month study, has alleged it has not received complaints, and because of this they continue to show what they believe people are watching. (Oakland Tribune, February 26, 1998.) In a more recent article by Parents Television Council (October 22, 1999, Oakland Tribune), it is reported that the National Institute of Mental Health and seven more national organizations report there is overwhelming evidence that violent entertainment causes violent behavior! In the Council's survey of 10 to 16-year olds, 62 percent said sex on television influenced their peers to have sex when they are too young. The Parents Television Council (the Hollywood project of the

Media Research Center in Burbank, California) is requesting that concerned citizens join them in their appeal. (See organizational list).

If you believe the motion picture industry should present "cleaner" or more family-oriented movies, you should write them. You are responsible for what your child sees! The networks, understandably, have freedom of speech; however, parents should be more concerned with what their children are doing during these early hours. Movies, at least, have PG-ratings to alert parents, and these ratings should be taken seriously. I must admit, however, that I have been to many "R" or "restricted" movies, where parents bring the children along. Because some parents also use the foul language, etc., they have no problem with their children hearing it, and some do not have a problem with the violence and sexual references. Though it might seem as if you are being overprotective, these are the informative years; those years where the child absorbs everything he/she hears and sees.

Some people are not aware that these ideas have a definite impact on children and teens. For example, if young boys constantly hear girls called derogatory names and are not told it is wrong, they will also refer to girls in that same manner. If a young girl sees violence within her family, or males degrading females, her views about relationships will probably be negative. In other words, she is more likely to grow up unable to trust, or choose abusive people to confirm what she is familiar with, or respond to disagreements in a violent manner; believing that confusion is normal.

Distinguishing Truth from Lies. There are many reports of alleged child abuse, especially when there is a custody battle involved. Sometimes the testimonies of children are considered "hearsay" and are ignored. Just recently, the California State Supreme Court broadened judges' authority to consider children's testimonies in paternity cases. According to <u>The Oakland Tribune</u>, December 30, 1997, "Court Deems Child's Abuse Story Reliable," when there is no physical evidence, hearsay is often needed. They cite a case of a three-year old girl who was seen touching her genitals during naptime at the preschool. The Aide is alleged to have told her to stop, and she replied, "My father always touches me right here." The girl lived with her mother following separation, and apparently during visits with her father, the sexual abuse occurred.

    The Commissioner ordered the father to undergo counseling and visit the girl only with a monitor present. Three years later, the father was allowed to resume visiting without restrictions! Hopefully this man has been cured of his illness, but in my opinion, all remaining visits with her should have been supervised. How does one know whether he will commit the acts again, or whether she will be killed for telling the truth?

    The Ruling (cited above) states that just because young children are unable to testify in court, this should not necessarily bar the use of their statements that appear reliable. The factors to determine reliability were as follows: whether a statement was spontaneous or prompted, language used, the child's mental state, and the lack of a motive to fabricate. In this particular case, the decision was made to use the girl's statements because she appeared to love her father and had no motive to lie, according to the report.

    The use of hearsay worked for all involved

in the above-mentioned case, however, there are many situations where a parent will instruct the child to lie, allegedly in order to prevent visitation rights or to receive additional money. An example of this, a high profile case in California, occurred several years ago. An eight-year old girl, who visited her father twice per month, told the school counselor that he played with her genitals. After a thorough investigation, and much embarrassment to the father, the child told someone that her mother had told her to lie so that she would not have to visit him. The father allegedly lost his job during the investigation. He said friends and family treated him differently, apparently because they were uncertain of the validity of the allegation; that he became very depressed. In fact, while sharing the story on television, he was very distraught. Crying, he said, "Once allegations of sexual abuse are 'pinned' on you, that even though it is later proven untrue, people still stare at you mysteriously, and you never live it down." This is outrageous, because not only does it trivialize the real cases where children report a father, mother, family member, or role model's violations; that father will never feel the same around his daughter or any other young female. In some jurisdictions this is changing; parents who are responsible for their children's telling these lies are now being prosecuted!

Though fewer cases are reported, boys are not exempt from unfound sexual abuse either. There have been several cases reported in Northern California where young boys were told to lie that the mother's boyfriend, stepfather, or father sexually abused them. In one particular case, the father was the promoter. He allegedly told the boy to lie and say the stepfather had molested him so he would not have to pay child support, however, he was caught. Sometimes parents (male and female) who try these tactics are not caught; there are cases where children have been abducted and taken to another country, or a mother or father who was only given visitation rights will escape there with a child.

There are also reports of sexual and physical abuse that are "made up" by the child without adults being involved. For example, one five-year old girl told her playmate's mother, "My father gets on top of me at night." The neighbor was shocked; stating she did not want to cause problems, so discussed it with a psychologist friend, who told her to share it with the girl's mother. After the mother spoke with her, without telling the father, the girl said she had seen a man on top of a woman kissing on television. The mother eventually shared the story with the father, and they both monitored what she watched.

If the above situation had not been handled properly with care and love as well, as a step-by-step process, it could have gotten out of hand. The mother was smart enough to investigate it further before accusing the father, divorcing him, etc., when the story evolved from television, and the girl probably just wanted love and attention from her parents!

The most difficult of these "lying" cases are the ones that involve teen-agers because sometimes they lie without encouragement. They do so for many reasons: because of jealousy of another person, dislike of a stepparent, low self-esteem, the desire for attention, or to hurt another person, etc. For example, many of you are probably familiar with "Eve's Bayou," an excellent movie which showed in 1997 involving a 14-year old daughter who knew her father (an alcoholic physician played by Samuel Jackson) was committing adultery. On one particular night he came home drunk, she sat on his lap, and the viewers only saw a brief scene of them kissing, and the father slapping her. The writer/director provided a very thought-provoking ending because it left you wondering whether he had, in fact, initiated the kiss. Most people agreed that he had not, but the scene evoked various discussions, some of which were: "The girl was trying to keep him away from other women in order to protect her mother," "She was a teen competing with her mother," or "She wanted her father's attention." Whatever the writer's premise, it did show how some teens will use ulterior motives for many reasons, and this can create additional conflicts in marriages, even when both parents are the birth parents.

Parents who are faced with situations similar to the above one should always use caution in handling them. You should listen carefully to ascertain the facts before jumping to a conclusion. Should you believe that your son or daughter has, in fact, been violated, do get some counseling. Some teens are too embarrassed to share what occurred in your presence, so it might be advisable to allow the child to meet with the therapist alone (after you have made the initial contact). If a family member is the alleged perpetrator, the entire family might require counseling.

Parents are also guilty of telling children to lie about abuse. Psychologists and courts use the phrase "parental alienation syndrome" or PAS to describe what happens when a parent tells a child to lie about the other parent. For example, a mother in California was ordered to stay 100 ft. from her daughter after she lied on the mother, who says she feels as if she has been imprisoned. According to the report, 90% of the cases involve women who are unable to be with their children because of the father's allegations (most of which are untrue). The child in this case allegedly did not want to go with her father but was forced. (NBC Report 11/13/00).

Effects of Spanking. I interviewed many adults, some of whom were "baby boomers" (teens of the 60's) who said they did not believe in spanking as a form of discipline. It was their contention that spanking causes children to become abusers, however, there are other people who disagree, believing that some abusive people were not spanked enough! My feelings are somewhere "in between" these theories: I did spank my sons, however, I did not beat them; there is a difference. Whatever your beliefs are regarding spanking, statistics do reveal that physically abused children have problems which have to be dealt with, otherwise they are more likely to do the same to others. It has been proven that some develop low self-esteem, become insecure, seek abusive relationships, and have problems in school.

Many parents believe spanking is the only thing that works! Some single mothers have reported how difficult it is to raise children, especially when there is no male in the home. For example, one mother of a three-year old girl stated she had spanked her because she had no patience. The mother said the girl had become so scared that she would "flinch" every time she saw her angry. The mother was requesting help because she had become afraid the spankings would turn into abuse. There are many more women who are now saying they are just too stressed to handle the children alone, combined with working and other household duties. More and more women are on the Internet asking other women for help. In fact, there are many chat rooms that are now focusing on these issues, and some cities have shelters and places where women can bring their children at no cost in order to take a rest. The mother who requested help was referred to Parents Anonymous and l-800-THE-KIDS. (See Organizational List.) Hopefully she received help, so that she would not abuse her daughter. At least she recognized the signals, which is an excellent sign that she probably did not.

The above-mentioned woman said she was too embarrassed to discuss it with her family, and afraid to see a counselor, fearing she would be reported to the authorities. It is sad when a mother or father, who is dealing with these stresses, feels helpless. Rather than asking for help, many become so overwhelmed with the day-to-day activities and parenting that they become depressed. Some have resorted to leaving the situation, killing the children, or killing the entire family and themselves! (In most cases this refers to males, however, there are situations where females have done the same).

Rather than beating the child, recognize that you might be a part of the problem and seek help. If not, your child might believe severe spanking or beating is the only form of discipline. What most people do not realize is, there are solutions, although the answer might now be exactly what one would choose; it is certainly better to reach out and ask someone than to violate another person to "save your face!"

Another reason some mothers and fathers beat their children is because they were severely spanked as children, so they only know one way to discipline. There are many reports of mothers who beat their children with belts and hot irons or lock them in closets because that is how they were treated growing up. Some of these children, if not counseled or given love, end up with severe problems. In fact, some actors have come forth to share how they were beaten, locked in the closet, and fed through an opening in the door! Others famous people have shared how they were treated by alcoholic parents.

  Recently I heard a story about a couple who allegedly locked their young daughter in the doghouse and fed her through the opening of the door as if she was a dog! Apparently she lived there until neighbors heard crying during the middle of the night. The girl, taken from the parents, was suffering from malnutrition. The parents, of course, were arrested, and the child removed. What would cause both parents to treat their own daughter in this manner? She will probably never get over the experience and will need a lot of counseling, so that she does not repeat the abuse on another person, seek out people who abuse her, or develop mistrust for everyone!

  Another horrific case occurred recently in Los Angeles where a five-year old girl was found in a closet drawer suffering from malnutrition! Apparently the couple's roommate heard her crying. It is alleged that when she was "bad" that the mother and stepfather would beat her and make her stay in the drawer! What authorities could not understand was, the couple had another child who was quite healthy. From what they could ascertain, the child was treated differently because she was not the father's. When mothers "go along" with the violations to their children committed by boyfriends and stepfathers, they are just as guilty and should be prosecuted as well! This child will remember this for many years; hopefully she will not parent in the same manner!

Child rearing is very frustrating, and even when you have raised a child; it is still difficult to enforce discipline with reason and rational approaches, according to G&S because each child is different. From personal experience, I am in agreement because there is no "prescription" for parenting. For example, my oldest walked at age nine months and was very easy going, while the second one cried all the time. Believing that he had a problem, I took him to the pediatrician, who informed me that because of my unhappiness while carrying him, it caused him to also be unhappy. The youngest, however, was also a very happy baby. Although all three were very smart children in school, the first two had more discipline problems than the youngest who apparently was too young to remember anything.

The most important factor in disciplining your child is to always keep love at the forefront, be consistent, while not allowing the child to take advantage of you. Many of you have probably heard stories about children as young as three years of age calling 911 to report their parents have abused them. Many parents now say authorities believe the children before they do the adults, consequently, some parents say their "hands are tied" when it comes to disciplining, and some are even fearful!

You cannot allow children to use this against you because you are ultimately responsible for them. In fact, there are people who are paying enormous prices in stress and money to get their children out of trouble because they were afraid to discipline. Whether you choose to spank, use the child psychologists' advice that spanking is detrimental, or use verbal or other forms of punishment, most of all, you must use wise judgment, show love, and be consistent in raising them.

Another method of discipline that some people are using but are not aware that it is abusive is to grab a child and shake it. According to many physicians and psychologists, this can cause brain damage to infants and young children. In a television show on "Parenting," a grandmother, who was keeping a four-year old grandchild, said the child would call her a vulgar name, and she could not get her to stop using it unless she shook her. Another woman was unable to stop her two-year old from throwing things or fighting, so to get her to stop, she would also shake her!

Another case of shaking involved a 30-year old man who received nine years in prison because he allegedly was angry with his girlfriend and vented this anger by shaking her infant son who suffered brain damage and is developmentally disabled! The child, at 15 months old, performs at a level half his age. (The Oakland Tribune, October 29, 1999.)

I am not making a correlation between the above-referenced cases to the following information, but it is very interesting. In 1998 Jeffrey Toobin, Legal Analyst for ABC, interviewed Dorothy Lewis, psychiatrist at Belleview Hospital in New York City. She had interviewed serial killers at the hospital, and autopsies revealed physical damage to their brains (frontal lobe) that could possibly cause compulsiveness. She said if these patients were abused as children, it could possibly cause rage in them. She further reported that injury to the brain at an early age creates impulsability and poor judgment. When Toobin asked her whether these children should be separated from society, she said, "That is the hard question!"

Scientists at the University of Iowa's College of Medicine have identified rare cases in which injuries to the brain in infancy prevented people from learning normal rules of social and moral behavior in childhood and adolescence. (The Oakland Tribune, October 19, 1999.) In an article, "Infant Brain Damage Affected Morals in Two Test Subjects," they discovered injury to the brain can alter moral judgment as well as one's ability to get along in social situations. A neurosurgeon, however, challenges this theory and states "If it is true that the human brain has a special circuit for learning right from wrong, and that circuit is faulty at birth, it would seem that changes in psychology and the criminal services would have to be revised. In other words, if injury to the brain can alter moral judgment, that should be taken into consideration

There are many tragic reports of infants dying from being shaken. One day care operator was sentenced to 25 years to life for allegedly shaking a 13-month old boy to death because he wanted to watch television rather than get his diaper changed! (The Oakland Tribune, October 2, 1999.) Other than the above-mentioned opinions, I found no other research to confirm or deny the theories, but I must admit, as a "lay person" I would not rule out either of the findings.

Emil Authelet, author of Parenting Solo, stresses the importance of understanding and controlling your temperament when you are disciplining a child. If you are upset or mad, you might do something that you are sorry for later. For example, some people will throw whatever is near in order to get the child's attention. Others have been known to slap the child as punishment. Both of these tactics are considered abusive! Some parents are inconsistent in their parenting: they only discipline if they are unhappy, however, on other occasions the child can "get by" with the same thing on another day and not get punished! That is sending double messages which children do not understand. If you are not consistent, children who do not receive help will also parent in this same manner. When you are having problems in your relationship, your child might "act up" or do something to get attention. Try to understand what they are going through because research reveals, as noted earlier, that children do love the abuser!

    Discipline should be a continual part of the growth process in order to teach self-discipline and respect. When the family is out of control, you should understand, without allowing the child to take advantage or use this time to be unruly, that he/she is also acting up. Everyone should practice self-control, and it has to start with the adult who is also responsible for his/her actions. Because maturity begins with self-discipline, it takes responsible people to make up a society and a family. When you do not use any form of punishment, you allow one person to infringe on the rights of another. Children should understand at an early age that actions have reactions, and they are responsible for their actions. They should understand that you some form of discipline will be used.

    When we refer to discipline, we are not speaking of physical violence or even spanking. It involves teaching rather than a physical act, in other words, letting the child know when he/she has committed an act that is out of line. There are other forms of punishment that is advisable, for example, discontinuing the child's television time, privileges, allowances, visits to friends houses, or other social outings. According to child psychologists, this has been proven to have more impact on a child than hitting or spanking.

Understanding the individual needs of each child is of utmost importance because some children will tell you exactly what is on their minds, while others are more private. Knowing each child's personality will help you determine how to discipline, while being nurturing, without denigrating the child's self-esteem.

Fathers must become more nurturing and caring as males, which is the opposite of violence. When male children see this, they grow up to be men and fathers who are nonviolent. Fathers should, however, set limits with children, because, in many cases, they do not always know how to control themselves, because the father and mother have not been role models; they argue or fight rather than talk to each other. G&S have probably conducted more research in the area of spanking of children (over 20 years) than any other researchers, and they are convinced that society must not spank if it is to prevent violence.

Sex Role Stereotyping. Society sends very different messages to boys and girls, which is referred to as sex role stereotyping. Parents and teachers are both guilty of this. In order to get rid of violence, this must be changed. Girls should be taught and treated just as boys are, in other words, counselors should direct them toward the same classes as boys. Conversely, boys should be allowed to participate in classes normally set up for girls and should be taught to be sensitive and caring; that it is perfectly normal to cry, hug, kiss, etc., or show emotions. (See the section on Male Abuse).

DOMESTIC VIOLENCE:

According to the Commission on the Status of Women, San Francisco, the FBI estimates that one woman is beaten every 15 seconds by their husband or partner in the United States, and between 2 to 4 million women are battered each year! The U. S. Department of Justice also reports 50 percent of women who appear in emergency rooms are victims of domestic violence. I was a victim of domestic violence in my first marriage, however, I believe I am alive today because I chose our lives over materialistic values! I made the decision to leave my job, my beautiful home, furniture, clothing, friends, etc., and move to another state along with my three sons who were ages five, three, and 18 months old at the time.

G. Miller, author of Violence By and Against American Children, states when comparing delinquent and non-delinquent youth, family violence or abuse is the most significant difference between the two groups. Einat Peled, et al, confirms this in a report entitled, "Ending the Cycle of Violence: Community Responses to Children of Battered Women." It is their opinion that children who witness violence at home display emotional and behavioral disturbances as diverse as withdrawal, low self-esteem, nightmares, self-blame and aggression against peers, family members, and property. Although my sons did not display any outward signs, my oldest suffered from bedwetting until about age eight, and the second one cried a lot until age four and got into petty trouble at school, and the youngest, age 18 months, of course, was affected the least.

Businesses are also affected significantly

when someone in the family is abused. In a report sponsored by Blue Shield of California, et al, San Francisco, they say domestic violence costs businesses between 3 to 5 billion dollars a year! Although many will disagree with their statistics, they report 95 percent of intimate partner abuse to be men against women, and victims are as likely to be found in boardrooms as on the assembly line. Because their research has shown that insurance costs in Corporate America are increased as a result of domestic violence, and 74% of women of battered women are also harassed at work, they have developed a program to educate and reduce violence. Not only is this program offered to employees, it is also available to business customers. We must commend Blue Shield for their proactive role. (See Organizational List.)

In order to break the cycles of violence, we must continue to educate and empower as well as provide avenues for assistance. Most researchers and others dealing with children will agree, the majority of children reared in violent homes grow up with some type of problem, for example, low self-esteem, drug and alcohol, criminal behavior, psychiatric disturbances, etc. Because there is not enough evidence to reveal that these effects are directly correlated (children reared in safe environments also have similar problems) one has to consider other factors, for example, economics, mental health, etc.

Whether a child is temporarily or permanently damaged, as an intellectual society, we are not doing enough to counteract this dilemma. According to B. E. Carlson, over three million children are at risk of exposure to parental violence each year. We must emphasize that this is "parental" violence - not from strangers! Economic pressures sometimes cause parents to hit or beat children. Stressful situations cause parents to abuse children and each other. The more problems, the more likely it is that parents will be abusive. Violent parents are likely to have been involved in violence as children, but not all violent parents were raised in violence. There is the risk that a violent past will lead to a violent future according to G&S, whose research showed no difference in Black and White families regarding domestic violence. (I did not ask questions regarding race, so have no statistics.)

Larger families had less violence than smaller, says G&S; families with eight or nine children showed no violence at all, because older children at home assist in the care of the younger ones, which took some of the stress from parents. Extended family was a valuable asset to families, however, today, they are almost non-existent in most families. (Except in cases where some family members are replacing the parents who are either incarcerated or on drugs).

P. A. Langan, et al, in the report, "Preventing Domestic Violence Against Women," it is revealed that domestic violence totals 48% of all cases that are reported by police. In 40% of these cases reported to emergency, the staff did not discuss the abuse with the patients! Another case of negligence, according to C. Warshaw, author of "Limitations of the Medical Model in the Case of Battered Women," occurred in a major metropolitan emergency department that had a protocol for domestic violence. In 92% of these cases, the physician failed to obtain a psychological history, ask about abuse, or address the woman's safety!

What are the Signals? In recognizing the signals of abuse, it is imperative that you not stereotype anyone. Just because one person behaved a certain way, that does not mean another person will act the same, or in a similar manner. There is no one set of qualities that designates a person to be violent; however, there are patterns to watch for to alert you of potential danger. A report reprinted by WOMAN, Inc. entitled "Early Signs for Future Abuse" produced by The Duluth Domestic Abuse Intervention Project, shares very important information of things to watch for. They state many of the behaviors that society stereotypes women to interpret as caring, attentive, and romantic, are actually early warning signs for future abuse. They list the following examples: intrusion, isolation, possession, jealousy, prone to anger, unknown pasts, and disrespect for women as signals to watch for. They are explained as:

Intrusion: The abuser wants to know your whereabouts, where you are going, and with whom, as well as when you are returning. He/she will telephone constantly or shows up at a friend's house unexpectedly. At first you feel as if you are missed, you feel loved or cared for, but in actuality, these are signs of suspicion and distrust.

Isolation: The abuser does not want you to have friends or be around your family makes fun of any hobbies, activities, books, or clubs you are interested in. Some men will call their partner's female friends names like "sluts," "stupid," etc., and you are discouraged from doing activities without him. Some people feel wanted and needed when their partners devote all their time to them, when in actuality, they are being cut off from friends and family for some reason. However, when they need someone to help because he has abused them, there is no one around; another reason my ex-husband did not want me to have associations. (My family lived in another city).

My ex-husband had negative comments to make about any female associate I had; either they were not a true friend of mine, jealous of me, "trashy," competitive, or desired him. Even though I ignored him, I was not aware of his tactics or reasons for disliking them. Later I learned that he did not want me to have friends who might tell me about his "womanizing."

Possession and Jealousy: He constantly accuses you of sexual interactions with anyone in your life, monitors your dress, even your make-up! For example, statements like: "You look like a whore." "Don't show your legs; they are all mine!" These are not "terms of endearment;" they are derogatory ways to treat you like an object, not as a human being!

Prone to Anger: The person is easily angered, has quick mood changes, and the anger does not match the incident; it is out of proportion. Some men have been known to beat the pets in order to hurt their partner, other abusive males and females will tear up pictures of love ones. If you are five minutes late, the abuser gets angry and before you can explain, you are accused. Once you ignore these aggressive behaviors or overreactions, the next physical violent behavior will be acted out on you!

Many people will initially act as if they are so "in love," until you become comfortable with them, and then they will begin hitting or choking you "playfully," but the acts will eventually turn to rage. For example, one young woman said her boyfriend would occasionally choke her, but emphasize that he was not kidding. When he picked her up, after working as a waitress, because she did not have enough money, he proceeded to drag her by her hair, striking her with his belt, and kicking her. He "allowed" her to return to work the next night, and the beatings began a second time. She was able to escape under the pretense of turning the television down in the other room! It was later learned that he was on probation for beating another woman. He was arrested without bail. (You would think the woman would have contacted authorities the first day rather than returning to work and allowing him to again violate her.

In my own case, an example of an angry outburst occurred after he had invited his family over for Sunday dinner. Prior to their coming, I had alerted him that they were running low on diapers, and asked him to fix the washing machine. He responded that he would before the family members got there, however, he never moved. After the family came I asked him again, and he suddenly became irate. I can vividly remember it as if it was just yesterday because the behavior did not match the incident! Everyone was shocked; however, no one said a word. When he "stormed" out of the house to the store, I was both shocked and embarrassed. This was another of the red flags; I should have left the next day, with or without funds! When I suggested counseling to him, he refused, again becoming upset. Even with this emotional abuse, I remained for another two years!

<u>Unknown Pasts and Respect for Women</u>: Do you know anything about the person's past, family upbringing, or personal relationships? If it is a male, do you know his relationship with his mother or other women? Does he refer to women in derogatory ways or stereotype men and women? Does she refer men as "no-good?" She might have had a bad relationship with her father and has a dislike for all men. Had I questioned my ex-husband, maybe I would have known that he basically had a problem with independent women. I later learned that he blamed his father for his mother's natural death and eventually grew to dislike him. Apparently she expired when he was 14, and being the oldest child who was very close to her, he never got over it. Had I known these facts, it would have given me some indication as to why he acted as strangely as he did, however, this would not have stopped the abuse, and it would not have caused me to stay!

    Many people do not want you to know about the past, and do not care to know about yours. This could be a signal that there is something they do not want you to know, which could also be a possible deterrent. For example, some people will not tell you that they have other children, but after you are involved, you learn that they are either staying with another family member or their mother or father. It is your right to know, so that you can decide before it is too late as to whether you want to become involved.

    Not only is it the honorable thing to do; to discuss the children before you become seriously involved, it is a "must" because in some states both salaries are included in computing child support. In other words, if the ex goes to court for additional support, the total wages are used. That is exactly what happened in my own case in my second marriage. At the time we were not aware that she could obtain additional support. In other words, it was as if he had received an increase in his salary! After she went to court on several occasions, the judge finally set a ceiling stating she could not receive any more because I also had children. Although I was aware that he had two young sons, I was not aware that my wages would be added to his salary. Having the children would not have deterred me from marrying because I knew the truth, however, there are some people who have ulterior motives and will purposely keep information from you. Most of those relationships will not last!

Myths Society Believes about Abused Women:

Many people believe:
- battered women are machoistic
- they like being beaten
- they did something to cause the abuse
- they should not leave - especially when there are children
- they are helpless individuals
- Many will return to the abuser.

These statements are made by many people, your family, friends, ministers, doctors, lawyers, etc., however, they are untrue. No woman likes the degradation and humiliation of a battering relationship, says WOMAN, Inc., who assists over 1,500 females each year. Many have no place to go, financial resources, or emotional support. The worst part is that many do leave, get restraining orders, and some still face additional threats and/or killings when they attempt to leave. Their report states 95 percent of all victims are females, three out of five women will be battered at least once in their lifetime, and four thousand are killed each year. These statistics do not correlate with someone being masochistic or enjoying being beaten!

According to FBI's report from local law enforcement officials via the "General Statistics" Report, women who separate from their husbands are more at risk than married women or those who get a divorce. This shows the importance of either working out the problems or obtaining a divorce when there is violence in the household. Prolonged separations only reinforce the problems because some people believe they still own you, and others think there is still a possibility that you will return. Their reports, "Female Victims of Violent Crime," and "Violence Against Women: Estimates from the Redesigned Survey," are available from the Bureau of Justice Statistics Clearinghouse at 1-800-732-3277 or via the Internet.

Many men who are against violence of women will not speak up when other males discuss the issue of beating women. For example, years ago it was not uncommon to hear a male say, "I guess I will go home and beat my wife, I don't have anything else to do!" Other men would laugh, and those who disagreed were too afraid to speak up for fear that they would be considered a "weakling."

There are theories that the "Saturday-night beating" concept was derived from the 18th century. According to Brott's report, this "weakling" myth has been practiced in some countries since that time. For example, in France, if other men learned that a male had allowed his wife to abuse him, men were forced by the community to wear women's clothing and ride through the village sitting backwards on a donkey while holding his tail. In Britain, villagers strapped husbands to carts and paraded them through jeering crowds. Although I have no factual information on this, apparently men began beating their wives, or saying they were, in order to avoid these embarrassing situations. Violence, then, is only an outgrowth of this phenomenon, but it has to be discontinued! With all of our technology, intelligence, etc., many humans still behave worse than the "lower species!"

Who is at Risk for Domestic Violence? No one is exempt from violence. You would believe pregnancy would make a difference, but there are cases where a pregnant woman has been beaten and raped by a spouse or a stranger! WOMAN, Inc.'s report entitled "The Health Care Response to Domestic Violence" revealed there were between 8% and 26% of battered pregnant women who appeared in public and private clinics. This figure is much higher because many are afraid to report the abuse. In 1998 a man in Northern California raped a seven-month pregnant woman. He represented himself as delivery person bringing flowers to her home. After a nationwide search, he was later found working in another city across country, having returned to his hometown!

There is Hope. In recent years, some women are being discharged from prison or not sentenced as long due to the battered woman's syndrome. In fact, the Governor Gray Davis of California in January 2001 pardoned a woman who had served 15 years for killing her boyfriend (with ten years remaining) who had battered and threatened to kill her, according to family members. She was released because of the work of the National Paralegal

Defense League, her family, and the Governor. It is hoped that more court systems will also take the syndrome into consideration when prosecuting people who kill others after years of abuse.

Although you are never totally healed from domestic violence, you must go on. You might believe that you cannot, but there are so many people who are survivors, after being beaten so severely that you wonder how they are coping. One of these women, according to KCAL's network's report (October 20, 2000) has undergone the first reconstructive surgery after being beaten so severely nine years ago that her children did not recognize her. After spending 4-1/2 months in the hospital, she developed gangrene in her face. She is scheduled to have two or three more surgeries and is working as a counselor in a home for women. This woman is amazing; she did not give up, she is giving back.

Because so any women believe they are alone, some retaliate with violence, and in many cases they are incarcerated because they killed their spouse in self-defense after years of abuse. Many states have set up advocacy services for domestic violence victims and "hand-picked" judges who are trained in domestic violence to preside over these cases in New York, according to NEWSFLASH.

Society must become more concerned with domestic violence of females, in fact, H. A. Holtz, a contributor to "The Health Care Response to Domestic Violence," reports that out of 143 accredited U.S. and Canadian schools, 53% do not require medical students to receive instruction about domestic violence. There is progress according to this report; the Joint Commission for the Accreditation of Hospitals and Healthcare Organizations (JCAHO) requires that accredited emergency departments have policies and procedures and a plan for educating staff on the treatment of battered adults.

Some females, for some reason, recognize abuse early in life, while others - no matter what age - fail to know when someone is violating them! A lot has to do with upbringing, past abuse, self-esteem, etc. For example, my deceased mother, a natural beauty, shared with me many years ago how she had to leave several jobs as a 14-year old teen-ager because the husbands, where she did domestic work, would either flirt, try to touch, or date her. The one, which remains with me, and probably remained with her, involved an older man whose wife was ill. He advertised for a housekeeper, however, shortly after arriving, he literally chased her throughout the house, and my mother eventually was able to get out of an open door. When she told me this story, even though it occurred in the 30's, I was very disturbed! I wondered why a man would advertise for a housekeeper when he wanted a girlfriend or prostitute! Because my mother had several experiences with these types of males, she learned the signals of abuse at an early age. Although she needed the money to help support other family members still at home, she was intelligent and mature enough not to allow herself to be violated. Consequently, she taught my sister and I early in life about empowerment, even when she probably could not spell the word or did not know it's meaning!

EMOTIONAL ABUSE:

Years ago, most people did not report abuse unless they were physically or sexually violated, but because mental and emotional abuse has become so prevalent, law enforcement, attorneys, and courts are now taking them very seriously. Some people believe emotional abuse is just as horrific as physical or sexual, even though the victim was never touched, because this violation remains with the victim long after he/she has been healed from physical or sexual. In fact, some experts believe that emotional abuse is more pervasive. For example, at least 10% of the males I interviewed stated they were unable to forget the verbal abuse rendered to them as a child, but approximately 20% stated they suffered emotional abuse from their wives or significant other, and the words or acts remained with them.

Many children are affected (as discussed previously) when they grow up with dysfunctional parents, and even when they are not physically or sexually abused, many are emotionally violated. For example, a young man in his mid-30's stated he grew up with an abusive father. He said although he never hit him, he beat the mother almost on a daily basis and on occasions the older brother and sister. He is unable to sustain a long-term relationship because he cannot trust anyone, will terminate the relationship for no reason, or he will do something so to aggravate the woman so that she will call it off. This is a case where someone was not physically violated but was just as affected because others were. He said he had been through therapy many times but cannot forget the violence. Because the mother never divorced his father, who is now disabled, he is suffering from emotional abuse. I suggested that he should meet with his parents to let them know how their problem affected him, to forgive them, and to move on; otherwise, he would carry the hurt the rest of his life. I also shared how he could continue to "hold on" to the problem, but he would be the one most affected.

Female respondents in my research said emotional abuse was just as bad as physical or sexual, but the determining factor depended on who rendered the abuse as to whether there was lasting effect or not. Unlike sexual or physical abuse, emotional abuse, in most cases, might not be so easy to discern. For example, one participant reported she believed her spouse was so nice because she never had to work. During the process of being protected from the outside world for almost 10 years, he left her for another woman he had met in the workplace. She had obtained no education or training, had no friends, and was 40 years old. If was so sad because she had never written a check! She believed she had a great husband and because he handled the business, she believed she had a good marriage. This woman said she felt very betrayed and has not been able to sustain another relationship, because she is unable to forgive, forget, or trust anyone else. This is a perfect case of emotional/mental abuse. Although this man did not physically violate her, he controlled her, provided her with all materials, while cheating at the same time!

Paul Kivel (expert on male violence and workshop leader) author of Growing Up Male: Identifying Violence in My Life (and other resources) recommends that males in relationships should make a plan so that they do not become emotionally abusive. He tells them to think about three choices when they become angry and to choose one of them, that males learn early in life that females should take care of them emotionally, physically, and sexually. Many expect females to be available whenever they want them to, and some men will assert control by teaching, training, or punishing them, according to Kivel. The basic message that some males are sending to women is that they are less important, and men fail to realize that they've been trained to see women as inferior. Examples of the messages society sends to females are as follows: "Be polite, be nurturing, and be pretty," to list a few. He says women dislike it when men make "catcalls" or lewd noises on the street. Some men use emotionalism to pressure women for sex. For example, "Show me you love me," and "You can't leave me like this," are familiar lines some men use to exert control over women. When they don't succeed, they say, "She's frigid," "She asked for it," or "She meant yes."

Verbal Harassment. This is another form of emotional violence. Many people are not aware that words are very "piercing," and they can be very painful as if you have been physically or sexually abused. For example, one respondent said her spouse hurt her so much because he knew what "ticked her off." She had shared a childhood hurt with him (the children called her "bony maroney" for many years) which kept her in tears. She said even though she was in her 30's, it was still as painful as if she was still a child. Her husband would wait until they were with other people and then call her that name. When she asked him why he hurt her, she said he would vow not to do it again, but it continued for years. She said the marriage was great, other than the husband calling her this name in public. Because he refused counseling, she eventually moved to another city with a girlfriend, leaving him a note. She later remarried, had two children, and is very happy. Some people might think this is a minor problem, certainly not enough to leave someone for. Because she had been a "bruised" child, hearing the name, especially with other people around, caused her extreme pain.

Some emotional abuse is un-intentional, however, some children and parents call children names such as: ugly, dumb, fat, etc., and according to how sensitive a child is, this is just as abusive as committing another type of violence. Most of us are guilty of being tactless; however, more emphasis should be placed in regards to sensitizing children and adults in the area of name-calling and its lasting effects. Even children who are being "bullied" by other children are now being protected because this has become such a problem for young children and teens. According to Wendy Craig, psychologist who appeared on the <u>Oprah Winfrey Show</u>, (November 14, 1997), many adults do not want to hear stories about bullying, but she says they should listen to their children. Bullying used to be a problem which parents and teachers took lightly because it was considered teasing, however, boys and girls are now being bullied through name calling, harassment, fighting, and other overpowering-type actions. In fact, there are reports of boys killing themselves after being teased so much. Not only are boys guilty; girls are bullies also. One girl on the show said she was called fat daily and teased that she did not have a neck. Because the teachers did not help, she had to be transferred to another school. A 17-year old girl reported she choked another girl, cut a girl's hand with a knife, telling her that it would not hurt, and bashed another girl's head into a window. When she was asked why she did those things, she said, "Because I wanted some attention." After going through counseling, she is now counseling other kids on the effects of bullying.

    The psychologist said kids should respond to bullying the first time it occurs, and they should continually report it until something is done because bullies believe they have power. Children should also ask other kids to help, because bullies usually do this with at least one other person. Some children say teachers have been told, and they do not help, or they say, "Each person is for him or herself." One young man reported that lots of teachers don't see it as part of their job. Unlike what you might believe, counselors say teachers are responsible for the children's safety.

PART II
CAUSES OF ABUSE

WHY PEOPLE VIOLATE OTHERS

Effects of the Media. According to G&S, millions laughed when Jackie Gleason would say to Alice, "One of these days you are going to get a pow right in the kisser," while shaking his fist at her on the popular television program, <u>The Honeymooners</u>. Most of us do not realize that some fairy tales and nursery rhymes supported abuse. For example, the mother from the rhyme, "The Old Woman Who Lives in a Shoe," beat her children when she sent them to bed. There are many others that are abusive when you stop to analyze them. Think about "Snow White," who was taken out into the woods to be beheaded by the huntsman, and another fairy tale "Hansel and Gretel," where the children were left to starve in the woods by their parents because money was scarce. These are just a few examples of how violence is used, and we do not realize what we are exposing our children to.

It is the opinion of G&S' that violence is as "American as apple pie" because it is considered a socially appropriate means of solving interpersonal and international problems. For example, duels and fistfights have long been considered the "manly" way of resolving differences between gentlemen! Other examples are: the Saturday morning cartoons showing the coyote crushed by the road runner and heroes John Wayne, Clint Eastwood, etc.; those who were quick with their fists. There are many Americans who believe that good parenting requires some physical punishment. (See section on "Spanking.")

Children and teens watch television talk shows where children are abusive to parents, and soap operas show women fighting. There are female wrestlers, mudslingers, and "gang bangers;" in my opinion, none of these are role models for young women! Geraldo has had many shows where female gang members use guns, beat other people, and laugh about grabbing an older person's money! One girl said she was upset because a couple was driving a nice car, so she proceeded to pull a gun on the driver, drag the female out of the car, and insert an iron pole between her legs! In fact, females are becoming more violent.

In 1998 in New York City, a 15-year old girl beat her female teacher unconscious because the teacher had called the parent to discuss her scholastic status! I can never remember anything like this occurring when I was in school, nor can I remember it 20 to 30 years ago when my sons were students. While watching the nightly news a reporter (whose name I missed) said young women are committing crimes in some areas more so than young men! Violence has become a way of life for many women, some of whom say they have had to defend themselves; others are fighting rather than being violated, but some younger women are now initiating fights with females and males for no reason!

The Parents Television Council in Burbank, California ran an advertisement in many major newspapers asking for contributions in order to appeal to television sponsors to stop airing shows that lead to violence. (The Oakland Tribune, October 22, 1999. According to their report, in a survey of 10 to 16-year olds, 62 percent said sex on television influenced their peers to have sex when they are too young. The National Institute of Mental Health and seven other national organizations report there is overwhelming evidence that violent entertainment causes violent behavior. In an ABC network study, 22 to 24 percent of young felons imprisoned for violent crimes said they had imitated crime techniques learned from watching television programs, as reported by PTC. This group totals he number of contributions monthly and then notifies the sponsors of their results. In 1999 they state 35 sponsors cancelled their advertisements as a result. It is their goal to stop television from airing "sex, filth, violence, and sleaze" and put their dollars in decent, family-safe programs. (For further information see the List of Organizations.)

Changes in the Family Structure. Family situations are very different than they were when I was a youngster. It was very rare to hear of a mother abusing or leaving a child, and almost never, murdering her children. She was truly the "backbone" to the family! In fact, most people stayed married because of the children, and there were very few divorces. I am not saying that all of those marriages were happy, because they were not! When I was a child, the family entity was held in high esteem. This is no longer the norm, in fact, many of my friends were raised by a grandmother, aunt, or other family member.

When I was growing up, there were very few divorces. Some men would leave their families (called a separation) but for the most part, women would never leave the children. If she did, she was viewed as an "outcast!" The man, however, could have several different families living in the same town! Some children even knew their father was also the father to other children, yet nothing was said or done. The wife, for many reasons, just went along with it, and some acted as if the other family did not exist; but there were some women who even raised the other woman's children!

Another reason many women remained in marriages that were undesirable was that many women did not work outside of the home. The man was the "breadwinner," and in most cases, made the decisions. There were some males who were very controlling: they would not allow the wives and daughters to cut their hair, wear make-up, or pants!

In some families, women had very little privacy. Most females during that time did not discuss their personal business even with their mothers or sisters, who probably had similar marriages. So even if a woman did leave, in many situations, she would return home to her mother and father's house, but shortly after, either they would send her back home to her husband, or he would come and get her. In my mother's case, apparently her father was ahead of his time (in the 40's) because she shared with me that he had informed all of the girls to return home if their husbands did not treat them right! Maybe my parents' marriage worked because my mother knew she had a place to go if they could not work out the problems!

Many women in my small hometown did not speak up - they were not as vocal as my mother was. For example, she shared a story with me about a man who heard from another male that his wife had told some of their personal business. Her husband then prohibited her from visiting anyone or talking on the telephone! From what I understand, some females believed the other women were treated the same way; in other words, they were taught the male was head of household and was to be respected, even when he was wrong! I can remember my mother voicing her opinion or disagreeing with my father on many occasions.

This might surprise many of the readers, but the church was where the majority of people in the Midwest and South spent their time. They attended at least once a week, and some people were there as many as three times and all day Sunday. Women played a majority role in the church, except they were not allowed to minister in the pulpit. (See section on "Religion.") However, they were allowed to cook, serve, and participate in the "circles" (a group that got together for a specific task like sewing, etc.), and other organizations, or belong to the usher board as well as determine ways to earn money for the church. The major decisions were left to the minister, deacons, and trustees.

The church provided a means of religious as well as social fulfillment (and it still does for many people) but in retrospect, I now understand that it was also a place where one could relieve one's frustrations. The church was a place where women and men could find their solace, because most were unable to do this at home! During the prayer service, the minister would ask if anyone needed prayer, and most women would go to the altar. In fact, some of the same people would go on every occasion. In retrospect, I believe they went for prayer on so many occasions and cried out loudly because they were living in abusive relationships.

Many women would discuss their problems at the circle meetings and other social functions. According to stories from my grandmother, mother, and aunts; there were many unhappy women, so these places became the places to share, complain, and gossip. If a husband found out that he was the topic of discussion, he would not "allow" her to attend the circle meetings again. If a woman told another woman that her husband was an abuser, and that woman told it, in most cases, she could not interact with her again. In fact, she was labeled as a troublemaker by some of the husbands.

During that time, a few women "ran the household" (made major decisions) but it was definitely a rarity. Most husbands did not want the wives to be in the company of an independent woman because their wives would question him or want to make changes in things she previously had no knowledge of. In other words, interacting with other women created problems within some families because they were no longer "in the dark!"

Most females during this period really had no social outlets other than these, except for the few who were considered "elitist" (a term used only by those who were not members) because they were members of the Eastern Star or other sororities. I believe my mother and several of her friends were exceptional: they were able to go fishing alone, shopping, and to take a night sewing/tailoring class at the junior college. I can remember, however, that one of the wives had to stop attending because her husband became jealous. My mother and her friend felt sorrowful for her and could not understand why because she was only making clothing for the daughters! They were not certain whether he was jealous that she was learning a skill, whether he thought men were there, or believed she was sharing their business! (Maybe she enrolled without asking him first).

In the early 50's the beauty shop was the other gathering place for some women, however, some men became suspicious because their wives would spend the entire day there. In fact, some would take their lunch. Just as the barbershop was the place where men learned the latest community news, some women would use the beauty shop for the same reason (a place to learn the latest gossip). Some males began going with their wives, but others would take and pick them up. In some cases, it was for transportation reasons; in other situations it was because he was jealous and controlling!

During the latter 50's as women began speaking out about their discontent, some began making changes. I remember one mother who left her husband with six children, moving to New York City with a girlfriend. This was the talk of the town because a woman had never done that! Women raised their children unless they were ill, an alcoholic, or prostitute. From what we understood, she was supposed to be "fed up" with her husband's womanizing, so she left abruptly, never returning.

Some families during that time had many unwanted children, and because it was the inception of the birth control pill, some females were glad there was a possible answer, however, some husbands would not let their wives take them. There are cases where the physician would ask the woman to bring her husband along for the gynecological exam so he could get the husband's permission. There are other stories about husbands' refusing to leave the examining room, so the wives could not be examined! Apparently one pregnant woman was not examined for the entire time she was pregnant because the husband was supposed to be jealous! These and other similar anecdotes support how emotional abuse can lead to physical violations and possibly death! There were many women who died between the ages of 30 and 40, who probably did not have to. Most were from untreated gynecological problems (some died from syphilis allegedly passed on from their spouse), illegal abortions that occurred in a disarrayed manner, cancer, and other problems that the family was too embarrassed or ignorant to discuss.

There are also stories of many women who had nervous breakdowns during the 40's and 50's and probably much earlier than that. In retrospect, many older females are now saying these women were sent to institutions, not because they were mentally ill, but because there were suffering from menopausal symptoms that were not studied by physicians. Many people attribute this to the fact that menopause is not a male's problem! It is my opinion that some females had nervous breakdowns because they were so controlled, lived in fear, and were unable to express their opinions. In other words, they had to remain submissive; consequently, they were not able to be creative or truthful! I also believe some died from stress-related illness and heart attacks caused by "broken hearts," (including depression, loneliness, etc.).

When women began exiting these relationships, many went to work in factories or performed housework (now referred to as "day work") because they were not trained for anything else. In the cities they were hired as live-ins which provided for additional money. Some even sent money home each week to the families to feed and clothe the children. As they became more self-sufficient, some women wanted their children to again be with them, and this sometimes created problems.

This brings us to the issue of unwanted

children: one of the main reasons that children are abused. The issue of unwanted children is a very "touchy" one, because it is difficult to determine who is responsible for the dilemmas we are faced with. Society has attempted to work on these problems, and many children are in orphanages, adopted, and in foster homes, simply because some people do not want them, cannot afford, or they are on drugs! In the United States, as well as in other countries, it is surmountable.

PART III

HOW TO ALLEVIATE ABUSE

THE ROLE OF COMMUNICATION

Is Silence Golden? There are occasions when both people should remain quiet, and times when one person should not say a word, simply listen. Even if you disagree, sometimes you should just hear the other person out. Conversely, there are times where silence is not golden. You might give the other person the impression that everything is okay because you are quiet. It is very difficult to know when to talk and when to listen. Getting to know your mate will be the key factor as to when you remain silent versus when you react.

What works for one couple might not work for another, and each situation is different. The important thing regarding communication is to be truthful and clear without demeaning your partner. It is still difficult (even in healthy or long-term relationships) to know when or what you should respond or not; experience will be the only teacher! Sometimes telling the truth or remaining silent is detrimental, however, the most important factors are; you should take the time to know and understand your mate and not assume that, that person is like the other person(s) you were previously involved with! You should treat each person as an individual.

Debating vs. Arguing. There are occasions when I have been in a discussion, and my mate believed that I was arguing, so I had to say, "This is only a discussion or debate." You should be careful that body language: facial expressions, gestures, and mannerisms don't mislead the person with whom you are talking because they do make a difference. If you are an expressive person, as I am, this could cause problems for some people, especially if the relationship is new. I am by nature a "demonstrable" person and use gestures in speaking with everybody, consequently, I have probably mislead many people. Previously I was not aware of the effect that gestures have on some people. Although I have not changed my personality, I am more sensitive to how body language can mislead.

Be careful that you do not use "fighting" words in any situation, unless, of course, you are prepared to leave! There is never an excuse to use them. This might provoke a person, who in the past has never been abusive. Because he/she is unfamiliar with your actions, it is possible it could be construed as becoming violent, and you cannot retract the hurting words. There are people who never forget demeaning, derogatory, or curse words. I still remember the one "B" word my ex-husband used during the five years, and that was 37 years ago, and he is deceased! In order to fight fair, you should consider the following:

- Use assertive language.
- Avoid name-calling, "hitting below the belt drawing attention to a person's known weaknesses.
- Stay in the present; don't dwell on past grievances.
- Listen actively and repeat back to your partner what you understood his/her thoughts to be.
- If you are wrong, admit it.

You Can't Argue Alone. My mother used to say, "It takes two to argue." That is definitely true! If you have a partner that uses arguing as a way to hurt you, then you must decide how much you can take. Some people definitely abhor arguing, especially when the person's voice becomes louder, because you are not sure whether that person is going to be physically violent. Some people, believing the person is getting ready to do bodily harm, will start fighting to protect themselves.

When I was a teen, a man in my hometown had a wife who would argue all the time. He came to my father for help stating he did not know what to do. If he remained silent, she would become very upset, if he said something, she would start a new argument and want him to respond to the new set of concerns. This would continue, and apparently the man became so upset because he was in a no-win situation. I am not sure what my father advised him, but he stayed with his wife until his death; hopefully it was not as a result of the stress!

You might be involved with someone who argues just for the sake of arguing. Most of these people are unhappy with themselves, and they want you to be upset. You will have to decide how much you can take if they will not get help. There are some people who want to argue because they want to attack you verbally, and there are couples who enjoy and thrive on this negativity. This is especially unhealthy for the children, other family members, and friends because the children will grow up behaving the same way. When I was married, there was a couple who fit the above description, and apparently they saved their arguments until they arrived at our house; at least that is the way it appeared. At first I tolerated them because he grew up with my ex-husband and had no relatives in the area, however, after several years of this (and our own arguments about their problems) I decided that I no longer desired to be in their company.

Tit-For-Tat. When you do something to get another person back; that is another form of illness. "Two wrongs don't make it right," an old adage which people referred to when I was young, is definitely true. In fact, problems start accumulating, and it gets to the point where neither person knows who did what, when. If you respond to your mate in this manner, the respect you might have had at one time will leave. Saving up hurts and hostilities and dumping them on your partner is not wise, and it certainly does not show love.

Talking Down. Another problem in communicating, which can be very demeaning, is "belittling" or talking down to your mate. There are some people who constantly do this, especially in the company of others. This is a definite signal that something is wrong in the relationship. You should tell that person how you feel, suggest counseling, or make a decision as to how much you can take! Some people will wait until they are around others to bring up personal issues. Rather than discuss their problems in private, he/she wants others to agitate the spouse. Then an argument ensues which the instigator wanted. This is no way to resolve personal problems. It embarrasses your mate, but it sometimes evokes other important issues, and this creates another problem! Maybe that person is not cognizant of what he/she is doing. Counseling might also help that individual if he/she will not listen to your discontent about "airing the dirty laundry" in front of others. If that person refuses counseling and continues to embarrass you, you are probably dealing with an abuser.

Using Sex as Reward or Punishment. This is a definite reason some people get physically and mentally abused and should be self-explanatory, but it is not, because many relationships are based on gifts or rewards in exchange for sex. Either there is love in the relationship, or it is not! Sex should not be used as a gift or punishment to hurt another person. If there is a reason that you do not believe that you should be sexual with your spouse, then you should discuss it as well as the reasons you have been "turned off" emotionally. If he/she has said something to hurt your feelings, and this has not been discussed prior to going to bed, it is understandable that you might not desire sex, however, this should be communicated. If that person is not aware, and asks for forgiveness, etc., then you should not continually use this same incident as a way to punish him/her. Some people will use it as an excuse to cheat when there are other underlying problems already going on. If communicating about the problem does not help, and counseling is refused, this might cause the demise of the relationship.

PART IV

WHY DO PEOPLE REMAIN IN ABUSIVE RELATIONSHIPS?

REASONS PEOPLE STAY WITH ABUSERS

Many people ask the question; "Why do people stay in abusive relationships?" What they don't understand is, 50% of women leave abusive relationships, according to Inform Editor, World Wide Web, January 14, 1997, in their report "Congressional Caucus for Women's Issues." When battered women leave their homes, they are frequently threatened with more violence or even death. Some face loss of shelter and much of their income, while others have concerns for their children because they risk violence against them or the possibility of losing custody. It is a very sad situation, when people have no choice but to leave, yet they have to take a chance on saving themselves and the children. I believe it is the only way, even with the adversity.

This book is not to alarm you as to how difficult it is to leave. What you must understand is: if you are currently living with some type of violence, be it emotional, sexual, or physical; leaving certainly will have to be better, especially in a long run!

Researchers and others working in the area of domestic violence, state that fear is the main reason most people will not leave an abusive situation. According to Mary Marecek, author of <u>Breaking Free from Partner Abuse</u>, fear is so powerful that it can keep you from saving your own life! Living should be the bottom line, the number one priority! Yet some people do not believe it and stay until they are killed or until they kill the abuser, in some instances, in the presence of children.

According to G&S, women who grow up in violent homes are more likely to stay with an abuser because they become tolerant of domestic violence or feel helpless, because it was what they learned as a child. In their research of 309 females, women who remained were less educated, had fewer job skills, and were more likely unemployed than females who sought help, called the police, or left. Again, money plays a major role in why females remain in abuse. In my research, 20% of women admitted they were still living with someone who was no longer abusive, while only 10% of men were with females who changed; the difference is, in most cases, men do not stay until you make a change!

Children needing fathers, even if they are abusers, is another reason some women say they remain. In my study, only 10% were still living with abusive men, and these women were either very young, with several young children, or did not work. The most prevalent statement in regards to children needing a father is that many women will say, "My son, especially needs a father. I do not want to bring him up without a man in the house," or "I did not have a father; I know what it is to be brought up in a broken home." What many people fail to understand is; if the father or role model is abusive, they are still living in a "broken home!"

Research has proven that children from dysfunctional homes can grow up to be happy, peaceful, normal adults if they have at least one good parent or role model, and that person can be another relative, friend, or foster parent! However, when children grow up in a dysfunctional household; most are affected in some way. Unless they receive counseling, many are guarded about entering a relationship, they have fear of becoming too close to someone, or they do the opposite; they befriend anyone, choose unwisely, and become violated again. Some people will seek out "weak" people or those with problems, hoping they will not be violated again.

There are many victims who believe the abuser cannot live without them. If you or the children have been beaten, and you choose to remain, you are saying it is okay because the abuser might not find anyone else to beat! By leaving, you might help the other person to get help, save his/her life, protect someone from going to jail, and possibly save someone else's life!

There are some women who use every avenue they can to teach the abusive spouse a lesson. For example, Lee Bowker, as referred to by G&S, conducted a survey of 126 females who admitted they had been beaten but reported the husbands had stopped the violence. These women had their own personal strategies: talking, promising, hiding, threatening, avoidance, etc., and they took advantage of friends, family members, neighbors, shelters, etc., as well as the police, lawyers, and social service agencies, etc. When G&S looked for a simple answer to how the violence was eliminated in a relationship (according to the above researcher) they were unable to come up with one simple strategy; however, the most important ones were determination and conviction. In other words, they were determined to stop the abuse! "Don't tolerate abuse; when you say stop you must be serious, mean it; if the situation gets close to violence, you should leave. Put yourself as Number One and do not assume blame for the abuse," says Bowker.

Knowing your abuser as much as possible is very important; however, this is difficult sometimes because some batterers have caught their victims off guard by surprising them or doing something out of context. For example, some abusers do not follow the cycle of abuse as referred to by the experts in this book. One female respondent said her husband, who had never been violent, beat her because he received a demotion on his job! She had no prior knowledge of why he was acting strangely when he came home from work. She alleges that he hit her for the first time, and she knew something was bothering him. He later explained why he was upset. Although she had nothing to do with his demotion, she ended up being victimized. Job loss has caused many, as stated previously, especially males, to become hostile and defensive.

Another female respondent said her husband would hit her no matter what she said or did. For example, if she was silent, he hit her for being quiet. If she talked, he hit her because he disagreed with whatever she said. She ended up leaving him, but he came to get her and after she was home, he beat her for leaving! Eventually, after saving a few dollars from food and other miscellaneous monies, she was able to leave, moving across country where her family lived. She said her only "saving grace" was that he was very fearful of her brothers!

Each person must decide "when he/she has had enough," in other words, no one can tell you when to leave an abuser. Reports are alarming regarding domestic violence; for example, a speaker at Domestic Violence seminar in San Francisco

(1997) reported that one out of every two women is abused! Due to this enormous problem, which society cannot seem to rid itself of, there are shelters, support groups, counselors, churches, etc., who are ready to assist. There are also legal advocates who will accompany you to court. (See the List of Organizations.)

If your partner is not treating you respectfully, you are not in a relationship anyway. You, of course, will be the person to make the final decision; however, many people are embarrassed to tell other family members and friends that they are having problems, so they continue to live in it until some people are eventually killed!

When It's Time to Leave. It is very sad when you cannot have the peace you are entitled to. Because of this, many women are constantly running, many out of the country because they believe the abuser will eventually find them. You do not have to suffer, as many women did years ago. There is help. Once you recognize that you are dealing with an abuser, you have to decide whether it is worth trying to obtain and/or suggest counseling. In my case, my ex-husband would not get counseling. He would say, "No one can tell me how to rum my family or live my life!" Consequently, I had no choice but to make preparations to leave. I called my mother in California, and with the financial assistance of my brother, she came by train to get us.

Your first concern should be regarding money. As soon as you realize that your mate is abusive, you should start a savings account, even if it is only $10.00 a week. You should always have taxi fare should you need to exit immediately. You should also have money for food and telephone calls. Many of you might remember the famous singers, Ike and Tina Turner. He allegedly left her in Las Vegas after beating her, and all she had was a gasoline credit card! She eventually was able to get back to Los Angeles and divorced him. She has returned to her career, lives in Europe, and states she has met a wonderful mate!

If you choose to leave and believe there is potential danger, sometimes you will have to leave without anything as Ms. Turner and others have. In fact, it is sad to report that some have left with only the clothing they have on their backs, but many are alive to talk about their experiences as well as to help others.

Next, according to Albert R. Roberts, D.S.W., et al, author of <u>Sheltering Battered Women</u>, you must decide in whom you can confide about your whereabouts. You do not want to share this with someone who might tell the abuser. You must be as careful as possible that you do not involve others in your domestic affairs, especially if your mate is a violent person. There have been cases where family members and friends were involved in a fight or killed because they tried to help the victim.

Another very important fact is to alert the school, principal, teachers, counselors, and yard supervisors that no one is to pick up your children except those people whose names you provide, because some abusers have come to the school to take the children and have been successful.

You must choose life at whatever cost! Don't listen to others when you know it is time to leave. They are not the ones being beaten, called names, or being cheated on. Use your own gut feelings about leaving. One respondent said that her mother lived with her abusive father for 30 years, but when she left her husband because he was abusive, her mother told her to take the children and go home to the abuser! Because she was not working, she returned, and the conditions worsened. Many years later, she moved out with the teen-agers, but it was only after scalding the husband in his eyes! This is very sad; however, her mother was so addicted to her own negativity that she did not understand that her daughter was in pain.

When I moved to California after leaving the abusive ex-husband, my Dear Grandmother whom I dearly loved said, "Honey, you should go back to your husband; he's a good provider!" Because she was of another era and deeply religious, it was so sad that she did not understand that he was a womanizer, physically abusive, and an ill man, and that I was also a "good provider!" Because I did not want to try to educate, disrespect, or argue with her at age 70, I simply explained, "Grandma, we are not compatible!" She never said anything more about him; she just continued to help with my three sons until her death a year later!

Many people recommend hitting back, however, G&S indicate that fighting fire-with-fire probably will not help a battered woman. Most people who are knowledgeable about domestic violence do not recommend fighting as a way to alleviate family violence. One female, referred to by G&S, stated she was surprised when she hit her husband back but was not surprised when he hit her again. The authors believe negotiation works better than emotional or physical fighting. They recommend mediation (conflict resolution techniques) and family counseling for couples.

Do not become used to or comfortable with

abuse! See it for what it is and do not call it anything else, or you will begin to make excuses for a dysfunctional relationship. An old American Indian proverb says: "If you allow a ghost to chase you, it will chase you all the days of your life. If you turn around and face it, it will disappear!" The first step is to recognize, isolate, and remove abuse from your life! According to Marecek, you should remember the following:

1) You did not cause the attack
2) You cannot keep it from happening again
3) Your words/actions do not influence his
4) Alcohol does not cause violence - it is the excuse one uses to be violent
5) Saying "I'm sorry" does not excuse what someone does
6) You do not belong to another person - you are not a possession
7) No one should be called "King" or "Queen" of a castle as an excuse to abuse
8) Whatever someone does in the privacy of their home is not okay if it is abusive
9) You are free to manage your own life.

Some people would prefer not to make a change, though they know it is harming them and the children, in fact, they would rather stay in a familiar situation with the negativity. Sometimes officers, counselors, and others involved with domestic violence issues, are unable to help because the victims are afraid to make a change. Ultimately, it is up to the individual, but in most cases, the police and others are called on many occasions before a decision is made to leave.

Another reason some women stay is they do

not expect abusers, rapists, or other abusers to be punished. In fact, 25% of the respondents interviewed for this book listed this as the reason they stayed or returned. Many women do not trust the criminal justice system because the victim is sometimes blamed for the crime. Even though many women are affected, many states are becoming more sensitive to domestic violence. Because females have been abused for many years, and a majority say nothing was done, more than half of battered women don't report their abusers.

Up until the twentieth century, men were able to "chastise" their wives without any type of law to deter them. It was not until the '70's that laws were implemented for women to obtain protective or restraining orders against abusers. It was around this same time that aid was provided to support emergency shelters for battered women. This led to a change in legislation to convict abusers of violence within the family. The protective orders were very helpful, as many wives preferred to use this rather than prosecute the abuser. As helpful as they have been to most people, these orders do not always stop men or women from abusing; so some cities are now training their forces to be more sensitive to the issue of domestic violence.

There are other reasons people do not leave. Some people love the intensity of their spouse's feelings, some are in denial because they grew up in chaos, others suppress it, and some become addicted to conflict (see the section on "Addictions"). I'm sorry to report, some people stay because they are "gold diggers;" they like the extra rewards they receive and would rather jeopardize their lives or the lives of the children! For example, one male said he cheated for almost 20 years, and even though his wife knew it, she would not say a word. He said when he had his heart attack, she would not give him a glass of water or drive him to the hospital, and he almost died! Do not remain in an abusive relationship and use tactics to hurt your abuser. Taking on another person's evil ways is not healthy!

      Do not stay in an abusive relationship and allow yourself to build up animosity so that you commit an act causing you to be incarcerated! The lady who poured hot water in her husband's eyes was asked why she did not leave. She said her attorney told her if she abandoned her house, she might lose it. (Some states have laws regarding leaving the premises). You should know what your state's rules are, however, do not remain if you believe you will be physically attacked or killed. Each person has the ultimate decision, however, in my opinion, leaving the house with the children was the best decision that I could have made - and much better than my being in prison or being killed. Some women, because of years of abuse, are now serving time in prison, even though they allege it was done in self-defense. Some of them, in essence, are serving time for the abuse that their husbands rendered to them!

      Your attorney and others might advise you to stay because of a Law, but you should make your own decision - you are the person who is being violated. There are many cases where women stayed with an abuser in order to keep the house, or because they wanted their children to stay in the house, but were later confronted by the physically abusive spouse! More and more this is the norm rather than the exception! I am grateful to the Denver Police Department, who inquired as to whether I had relatives in the area, and informed me that I should leave my abusive husband permanently.

Initially I was upset because I believed the children and I were being treated as victims because we were being asked to leave! I cannot thank the Denver Police Department enough because they were sensitive to the issues of domestic violence much earlier than most cities. The officer had spoken with my ex-husband, so it was probably something he said that caused the officer to tell us to leave. I followed his advice, and we are probably alive today as a result! Conversely, it has been said that many in the legal field are unsympathetic to females even after years of beatings, etc.

Matthew Litsky, researcher and author of Reforming the Criminal Justice System Can Decrease Violence Against Women, cited in David Bender's book <u>Violence Against Women</u>, states many police are trained to mediate rather than arrest the abuser, and many non-enforcers believe the old tradition, "a man's house is his castle." Many officers want to respect the privacy of families, so do not get involved. Prosecutors must not dismiss these cases, and judges should not simply lecture the male abusers, even if it is the first offense. The abuser should not be freed on low or no-bail, and judges should not convey, what many people believe, that society condones domestic violence of females!

There is disagreement, however, with Litsky's opinion that removing abusers from the home reduces violence, because there are many situations where that person has returned to beat and/or kill the victim. The Crime Control Institute, an organization in Washington, D.C., according to

Bender, states little is known about individual effects of incarceration.

From their research, full arrest did not have any effect on employed people, and it had a criminogenic effect on unemployed people. Although each community differs in the misdemeanor length of time, according to the report, approximately 1/2 are released between one day and one week, and some only stay one hour, giving the abuser time to return to the victim and commit more serious violence. For example, in 1996 a San Francisco woman was beaten severely by her husband for obtaining a restraining order. When she went to the police department, he followed her and began beating her again in front of their office! While the victim was hospitalized, the abuser set the house on fire, burning it to the ground! The woman eventually had him arrested, but apparently he was only held for a brief period. This person does not appear to be afraid of the law. Hopefully he received a life sentence, otherwise this woman should move to another city because he will eventually kill her, or she will kill him in order to protect herself.

I believe short arrests only tease most abusers because it is not enough time for them to learn a lesson! It is also the opinion of the Crime Control Institute that short arrests are not painful enough, their lifestyle is not disrupted, and they can still return to their jobs. On the other hand, they state that although incarceration disrupts; it does not deter and sometimes backfires on the victim or society. In their one-year experiment, suspects took short custody (2.8 hours) more lightly than long custody (11.1 hours). (Long custody?) They believe a little jail time can be worse than no time at all, however, certain types of offenders are not affected by any arrest. The group does not disagree with mandatory arrests; however, it is their opinion that other types of legal intervention would be far more beneficial regardless of time, especially with underclass populations.

According to G&S, sometimes the community agencies and practitioners feel a greater urgency for change than the families themselves. In many occasions the abused person does not want assistance or therapy, and the entire family is left without help because the abused person's agenda is different than the person assisting. In fact, in one study, it was revealed that 97% of victims said they still loved the offender! This leads us to the next section; addicted to negativity.

Addicted To Negativity. According to Robin Norwood, author of Women Who Love Too Much, some women are addicted to pain and familiarity of an unrewarding relationship with an abuser. Most females affected by this disease developed it during childhood. Because it is difficult for some women to figure out that they love too much, the disease is becoming severe, costing many women their lives! According to Norwood, it is similar to a heroin addict quitting "cold turkey;" the victim must allow painful feelings to come because the body and emotions need healing.

There are those victims who seek abusive-type people, even platonic friends. Some of you will be shocked to read this. For example, all of us have known people who meet a nice person, but because there is not enough conflict in the relationship, they terminate it and eventually end up with someone who will fight either mentally or physically with them! These people are not happy until conflict occurs. Most are victims of abuse from a youngster, others have more severe psychological problems (neurosis, psychosis, character disorders) and some suffer from a physical illness.

There are also those people who allow abuse for so many years, who end up very bitter. These are some of the same people who say; "relationships don't work." They put everyone in the same category and, because they remained in the situation so long, they do not trust anyone. Most have never received therapy or tried to find ways to heal. Victims who do seek therapy, who have multiple crises and history of chronic and severe problems, often defy practitioners who try to help them. They make statements like; "You don't understand," or "No one can help." Some of these people are so addicted to abuse, and many are unable to determine what is abusive and what is not.

Deepak Chopra, M.D., author of <u>Ageless Body, Timeless Mind</u>, states that many people believe they don't have a choice in what happens to them because they are so addicted to negativity they cannot see themselves out of it. It is imperative that children be given a choice - even if the adult has an addiction problem!

Women who remain in abusive situations have certain characteristics, according to Norwood, as follows:

>1) They did not have parents who were caretakers who loved them.
>2) They have not had love, so they are willing to wait, work harder, and hope.
>3) They don't believe they deserve to be happy and must earn the right to enjoy life.

4) They choose wrongly, because most people choose externally. (Most of us are guilty of this).

Many people, especially females, get involved or fall in love too soon, without knowing anything about the person. For example, Deborah Gregory, in her article "Who is That Man," states there are "red flag" or warnings to let you know when something is wrong, and your radar should automatically kick in. She said you should keep an eye out for the bad apples and not enter into a relationship with a person you do not know anything about. In this society, according to Gregory, we are very careful about everything else that affects our daily lives, but we enter into relationships with people before we check them out, and getting involved with "Mr. Wrong" (or "Miss Wrong") is far more devastating and costly than being lonely. She said, "There are no 'Prince or Princess Charmings' coming to save you - just a lot of frogs!"

It is not easy to make the change to a new way of communicating with yourself because people become so addicted to negativity that they miss the fights and the making ups, etc. She cites an example of what some therapists refer to as the "Honeymoon." This is the cycle when the abuser makes up by buying flowers, making love, crying, etc., and after this is over, he/she abuses again, repeating the "honeymoon." She says even after the victim threatens to end the relationship, the abuser repeats this act until the victim or abuser leaves, or someone is hurt or killed.

In order to heal your addictions, you must first admit that you have one. (This applies to the abuser and victim). Realizing that you are addicted requires inner work, and you must look clearly at the places where you lose power in your life, where you are controlled by external circumstances. Authelet says once you acknowledge the addiction, you remove its power. As you start the healing process (although it might take years) you will gradually realize how secure you feel. During this process, there might be a period of loneliness because the negative behavior you are used to has been removed.

There will be thoughts of returning to the hostile or safe environment. It is very important that you find positive resources: therapy (group therapy is helpful), Alcoholic Anonymous, or a 12-step program - even if you do not drink - social functions like church, etc., and most of all, some type of exercise like walking, etc. Yoga is also very physically and mentally challenging. This is also a time to enroll in a class, attend seminars, or obtain additional training. In other words, you might want to add a new hobby to your life. Reading inspirational books helped me. One of my favorite authors, Gary Zukav, who wrote <u>The Seat of The Soul</u>, truly helped me in becoming "whole." It is one of the most powerful, fulfilling books I have ever read! Many people have never known or recognized the "true self" because they were victimized at an early age and repeatedly violated throughout their lives. Because they have never received help, most suffer from low self-esteem and continually choose negative behavior.

<u>Addicted To Love</u>. Peck says the second most

common misconception about love is the idea that dependency is love. This is a misconception which psychotherapists must deal with daily. In other words, people believe they cannot live without another person, believing that life cannot go on if the person leaves!

Love is freedom; when you require another person to validate or confirm you, you are being a parasite! In other words, love is the free exercise of choice. Each person wants to be nurtured at some point, but when you cannot experience wholeness without another person, apparently you believe that you have no real sense of identity because you are defining yourself solely by your relationship. One example of this occurred to an associate that I worked with years ago. From what we understand (according to her suicide note) her husband had allegedly told her that he was going to another city to seek work. She apparently realized that he was not coming back, because they only visited each other about once per month. She left a note to the effect that life was not worth living without him, then sat in a chair, shooting herself in the heart! It was a shock to her friends, family, and work relations because was a very professional executive secretary in her 40's, who had not shown any signs of mental illness. It is very sad when you allow yourself to be an appendage to another person! In order to be mentally healthy, you must believe that you are separate and equal; most of all; you should never give your birthright entitlements (power) to another person!

You should have your own set of values; continue to enjoy life with other friends and family, so that you do not become obsessed with anyone! When this happens, you are suffering from an addictive or co-dependent personality. M. Scott Peck, M.D., author of The Road Less Traveled, says these people are addicted to people, "sucking on them" or "gobbling" them up, and when people are not available, they often turn to alcohol or drugs as a people-substitute. According to Peck, one of his colleagues made the statement; "You would be better off depending on heroin, than depending on another person. At least if you have a supply of it, it won't let you down, and if it's there, it will always make you happy! If you expect another person to make you happy, you will be endlessly disappointed." And I agree!

      Passive dependent people crave for love as if starving for food. Because they have an inner emptiness which needs to be fulfilled, they always feel "part of me is missing," and because of their lack of wholeness, they have no real sense of identity. They are defined by their relationships. Peck shares a story about a man who was extremely depressed after his wife left because he would not give her or the children any attention. After threatening to leave several times, she did. He was extremely upset and was suffering from anxiety, seriously contemplating suicide. Peck was confused because the man had told him that the wife's complaints were valid. When he saw the man two days later, his personality had changed; he had met a girl the night before at a bar and said he felt "human" again, telling Peck that he would not have to be seen again! Rather than continuing to work on his problems, he immediately found another person to replace the wife. His man was suffering from an addiction and will probably repeat his pervious actions!

      Dorothy Corkill Briggs, author of Celebrate

Yourself - Enhancing Your Own Self Esteem, says too often we select partners and friends like the family member who failed to validate our love ability. If you choose someone because that person "rounds you out," it will put you in a needing, dependent, and ultimately a resentful position. It keeps you from being "whole," and if either person changes, the original basis for coming together is threatened. That is the reason so many insecure people choose people with problems; however, if the problematic person changes or starts working on him or herself, the insecure person no longer feels comfortable.

Passive dependent individuals change their personalities rapidly, and as long as there is someone to fill their void, they are temporarily happy. They do not take the time to heal or to analyze the true self, instead, they move on to find a replacement as the man, mentioned previously, did. People who are addicted to sex also fall within this category. Some women and men will go from bar-to-bar seeking people for relationships. They will not wait long enough between affairs to get involved with someone. Many are attracted to abusers.

Children growing up with passive dependency parents usually end up without inner security and seek attention wherever they can find it, and many of these parents depend on the children far too much for the love they should be receiving from a mate. Consequently, these children seek both discipline and love, and unless they receive help, they grow up to repeat the same lifestyle of the parents, and most will seek an abuser! As an adult, they become involved with anyone who will provide some type of attention, and many are killed either at the hands of an abuser and/or drugs. They die from seeking a false sense of security. Peck calls this anti-love: attaching yourself to another person. Ultimately, this will destroy you rather than build a relationship. Most secure people end up leaving a relation- ship where the other person is so needy, however, if you ask insecure people why it ended, most would say, "I don't know because I did nothing wrong!" They never realized that they were suffering from passive dependency or co-dependency.

    If you are living with a person with an addiction or co-dependency, you should suggest that he/she seek counseling. (By the time you recognize it, you might also need therapy!) If there is a child suffering from passive dependency, you should refer him/her to the school psychologist, counselor, or a therapist so that he/she can work on his/her self-image in order to become a more secure, independent individual.

    Zukav says accepting that you have an addiction is also acknowledging that you are out of control. Once you are whole again, you have to make time to listen to that inner voice. For example, before I began my healing or self-discovery process, I spent a lot of time dealing with abusive male and female associates, as well as employers, so I did not take time to listen to my own voice, which included analyzing my own and other people's behavior. In retrospect, I had become co-dependent to other people's problems even though my purpose was to help! What I failed to understand was, if I could not help myself, certainly I could not help anyone else. Many people expend so much energy, as I did, and until something traumatic occurs, most never realize the effects of their behavior, that their energy could be utilized in other more positive ways. Secondly, they do not realize that in their intent to help, in most cases, is truly reinforcing the other person's negativity, insecurity, etc., and sometimes they are using abusive acts in the name of help. Some helpers are also being abused.

Because many people are so preoccupied with being the "rescuer," "nurturer," "coordinator," and so-called "people person," as I was, their lives are spent reaching out, and they do not have any time left for themselves. Had I not left the stressful job, I probably would have retired (or died) there without ever discovering my true passion (writing) or my reason for being!

Loving too much is a progressive disease, which also results in stress-related disorders such as, strokes, heart disease, other illnesses, drugs and alcohol use, and violence. You should not look "outside" yourself, but practice discipline to build on your own inner resources to fill the empty or lonely feelings. Norwood gives the following steps for recovery:

1) Seek therapy
2) Make recovery your first priority
3) Find a support group
4) Develop your spiritual side through daily practice
5) Learn how to not get "hooked" into the games
6) Face your own problems or short-comings
7) Cultivate whatever needs to be developed within you
8) Become selfish
9) Share with others what you have

experienced and learned.

I would also add that you make time for some type of exercise. That does not mean that you have to join a health club, etc., but do whatever you enjoy. I prefer walking which is something I can do for the rest of my life. This will keep you from becoming stressed as well as provide the time for you to think. Sometimes when you are alone, you will review where you are in your life and work toward making changes.

Many people, however, will not seek help for many reasons, for example, they are embarrassed, they want to remain for money or materials, they are fearful, and some even believe they have failed! None of these have validity. First of all, most people during the lifetime will have a problem for which they will need assistance. This is not a sign of weakness. In fact, it is the reverse; it has been said that strong people are the ones who seek or ask for help, because are secure with themselves. When they recognize a problem, they look for solutions.

Do not use money as the determining factor. There are many free organizations, counseling centers, and others who charge on a "sliding" scale (according to your income). Also don't be too proud to share your problems or ask others of referrals of therapists. It is not recommended that you discuss your personal business with everybody or strangers, but most people are concerned about others. For example, people want to know if there is an abuser (especially a pedophile) living in the neighborhood. You might be living with a sexually-addicted person (male or female) who might be part of your local school district, church, boys or girls club, etc., and that person might violate or rape a child nearby.

You are just as responsible if you are aware of your spouse's problems. If you choose to stay, that is your decision, but if he/she molests someone, you might be considered an accomplice!

For resources for help (other than the organizational list in this book) the yellow s of your telephone book will help, as well as your church. Some jobs will pay for counseling, and others have therapists there to help. Do not suffer alone or add to another person or persons being abused.
Most of all do not remain passive, take a proactive role so that you are not a statistic! Be truthful, especially to yourself, seek help, and realize we are only human beings in a vast world that no one totally understands!

Becoming Co-Dependent. This is similar to "loving to much" or the passive-addictive personality however; it usually is caused by another person's problems. According to Dr. Charles Whitfield, author of Healing the Child Within, it is one of the most common conditions causing confusion and suffering in the world. These people, as discussed earlier, give their power to others. The co-dependent person is not aware that they are being set up for abuse; it just becomes a way of life for them. The horrible part of this problem is that co-dependent parents breed children that are co-dependent, and the cycle is repeated!

It is very important that you are able to recognize and delineate these problems. For example, Whitfield counseled a 45-year old female patient whose father was a workaholic, and her mother was a compulsive overeater. She had been taught to be a people-pleaser and self-sacrificer. Both of her husbands were alcoholics, and she never refused anyone. She was super-responsible, went back to college, worked hard, but became depressed. She took an overdose of sleeping pills and enrolled in Alcoholic Anonymous and group therapy for two years. It was determined that her mother was her biggest problem, because she used the daughter as an example as to how she was to feel. The father was absent due to his work, and the woman was still mad with her father for not being there when she needed him. This woman had developed a dependency because of an ill mother and missing father. She eventually recovered, stating she is now a new person: mentally, emotionally, and spiritually.

Many of your problems as an adult stem from how you were reared as a child, the interactions you saw, and how you were treated. Sometimes without therapy, you can break the "cycles of negativity" by analyzing each of your problems, the person(s) who caused them, and the possible reasons, however, most people will need some counseling at some point during their lifetime. As an adult, do not allow your codependent parent(s) to control you for the rest of your life (even if they are deceased)!

Personality Problems. Many people who are abusers, or who are addicted to abusive situations, suffer from neurosis or have character disorders. According to Peck, these two conditions are simply disorders of responsibility; the neurotic assumes too much responsibility, and the character disorder shuns responsibility. Neurotics blame themselves, and character disorder people blame others. If you will follow this analogy, you can clearly see why so many people fit within this mold. The worst situation, however, is when two of these people form a relationship! First of all they should not be together, and secondly, they do not make good role models. Because most women tend to fall within the nurturing category (the person who assumes too much responsibility) most blame themselves when the relationship is not working. But when a person suffers from some type of neurosis and is involved with another neurotic or a person with a character disorder, unless they get help, there will be problems. People with character disorders will blame everyone except themselves: for example, their mother, the job, the world, friends, etc., and will not admit they need help

Most neurotics also suffer from low-self esteem, and according to Peck, even their speech patterns are different than a normal person's. For example, they use words like: "I should have," or "If I could have." They are very pessimistic; many do not have very strong or definite personalities. These people believe they have no power, allow others to lead them, and unless they receive help, they suffer many years at the hands of abusive people. Some will require continued therapy in order to become "whole." Self-examination should not be considered embarrassing. The road to recovery is possible, if you are truthful! If that means taking medication for a short time - or a lifetime if necessary - that is the price of having joy in your life!

Children who grow up with pessimistic people, parents with low self-esteem, or other character disorders as described above will become ill-responsible adults unless they get counseling. Because the children will not have a built-in mechanism or conscience to let them know when they are wrong, many will go through life either abusing or allowing others to violate them. When people rape boys, girls, disabled people, or anyone; research reveals they were either abused as a child, born with a character or brain disorder, or were the products of parents with neurotic and/or character disorders.

I believe it is our responsibility to recognize as well as help children and teens and to steer them to medical intervention. Many people reach out to others so they won't be victimized again! They do not realize that that sets them up to be violated repeatedly. In my case, I was not a true codependent, but was more of a nurturer because I patterned after my mother and grandmother, who came from a patriarchal society. My grandmother believed men were heads of the household and no matter how they acted, the woman was supposed to listen as well as follow them! My mother, on the other hand, believed differently, even thought she grew up in a time when most females did not voice their opinions - especially publicly.

As I began my self-discovery process (which took years) I began reviewing my life, analyzing my past, and re-evaluating my upbringing. I decided there were many good qualities and morays that my parents, relatives, and role models had taught me, but there were some that I wanted to "bury!" With no disrespect to my dear grandmother, the first one that I dismissed was the myth that the man was supposed to be head of household (especially when many are not there and did not rear the children) or did not bring his paycheck home, etc. I realized that many of the "old morays" that I had grown up with had, in fact, contributed to my becoming a nurturer, co-dependent, or caretaker. I also realized in order to "reclaim my birthright" that I would have to revise some of my behavior! (My mother must have also realized this).

The next part of my self analyzing was to get rid of the negative people who had excess "baggage" (people who complained constantly but would not do anything to make changes, who were destructive or would never say anything nice about anybody). In fact, they were depleting my positive energy! But I had to also realize that I was part of the problem because I allowed them to "dump." It took about ten years to do this because there were so many associates and so-called friends who were relying on me as a therapist, etc.

It was almost as if I had become a new person. (It is sad that I did not understand this until about 45 years of age!) Although I had had an enjoyable life, accomplished many things, and contributed to many people, in retrospect I was not happy with myself. What I had not realized was, my life was filled with quantity rather than quality!

Choosing Between You and the Children. Once you decide you are with an abuser, do not use the children as an excuse to remain. This should not be a choice! As Authelet says, "If you are on an airplane, the steward always says put on your seat belt first, then your child's. In other words, you are the child's lifeline. In order for the child to survive, you have to live!" If you remain in an abusive relationship, you are allowing your child to be emotionally abused, and also taking a chance on both of you being killed!

Authelet also stresses the importance of nurturing, caring, and affection, and I believe my sons are alive today because they had tremendous amounts of all three of these from the time of birth until they left home. Because the lines of communication have always remained open, they understand, should they have problems (even as adults) that I am always available to discuss any subject. Openness, honesty, maturity, and love are the concepts of good parenting, and these qualities will be of utmost importance during these stressful times. Authelet says you should not believe the myths of single parenting, such as:

"**You are a broken family**." - This is not true. Being a whole family has nothing to do with the number of parents in a home or the marital status. Whether your family is comprised of a single head of household, mother or father, etc., it is whole, entire, and complete.

"**Your children are disadvantaged**." - Authelet says the latest statistics show single parent families are producing excellent achievers, and it may be because parent and child now depend solely on each other. He doesn't negate the fact that some children have suffered following a separation from one parent, but says others have "blossomed" after a divorce, when they were not able to before because of the negativity within the family!

"**You are a loser because you're divorced**." - Do not believe this statement. The old adage "misery loves company" might apply here. Some people will tell you this because they are too afraid to leave. They are miserable or jealous because you are happier. Once you have made a decision to leave, do not listen to anyone who tells you to stay in a hostile environment!

Save the Children. Children are 12 times more likely to die by the hands of gunfire in the United States than any other country, according to NBC's report of February 7, 1997. David Rubin confirms this in his Time Inc. report of 1996. According to the U.S. Advisory Board of Child Abuse & Neglect, child abuse is on the rise! He says five children in the U.S. die at the hands of their parents or caretakers. This report was so shocking that they titled it, "A Nation's Shame." We should all be appalled, especially when they report that figures for abused or neglected children might be low because health officials don't always recognize it, and police don't always fully investigate these allegations. Their report shows 18,000 children a year as permanently disabled by abuse and 142,000 are seriously injured! Due to the failure to recognize this abuse, 85% of child-abuse fatalities are mistakenly identified as disease-related or accidental!

The Advisory Board is to be commended. Their priority is to train health care workers, social workers, police, and teachers to recognize and report abuse. They also recommend tougher laws for prosecuting people who abuse children as well as accelerated prevention programs. It is a sad situation when children, of no choice of their own, cannot pursue or enjoy their birth, civil, constitutional, or any other rights because we cannot recognize a potential abuser, we choose wrongly, and when we do get involved, we do not have the where-with-all to leave!

Many people said they stay with an abuser because there are children, however, it is the most crucial thing you can do! According to Cooney, there is so much that society has to learn to better protect children from abuse. The attitude that children are the property of their parents must be changed! Children should be explained why a separation is needed if they are teen-agers; however, it is more difficult when there are younger children involved, as they do not understand why mother and father are not together. Even in cases where they are too small to know the particulars, you should still not remain in chaos until something happens to both of you. Eventually they will, in most cases, respect each parent for attempting to provide peace in their lives, and if they don't, at least they will be alive!

My oldest son, at about 14 years of age, attempted to blame me for leaving his abusive father. I had not explained to him in detail the abuse rendered to me because I did not want him to dislike his father. Because I did not share anything with him, he believed that it was my fault for leaving his father's family, his beautiful house, etc., and proceeded to tell the other children untruths. I understood that he was very hurt but too young to understand. I tried to explain to them that we were separating because we could not get along. I don't believe he understood until he was in his early 20's. He telephoned his father, who lived in another city, to ask for monetary assistance, but instead his father cursed at him. He telephoned me crying and asked, "Why didn't you tell me my father was that way?" He had never asked his father for anything but when he did, he received just a portion of what I had lived with for five years! My oldest son and I are the best of friends now, and he has thanked me on many occasions for being the only person who has been there for him during his problematic times.

It is so important that you make wise and expedient decisions regarding you and the children.

Once you make the decision to leave or divorce the abuser, do not be dismayed or question yourself as to whether you made the right decision or not. Even when children are blaming you or acting out of control, do not say "I wish that I had stayed," because you might have remained and been killed!

Remember, there will always be problems that the children will not understand, and certainly they will be temporarily affected. For example, one respondent, after divorcing, had a son who began urinating in the bed from age eight to age 12 years. The doctor told her that he missed his father and his familiar surroundings. She said she blamed herself and felt responsible for the child's problem, but what she did not understand was, she was the person responsible for the child being alive! After he received counseling, he was happier, and his grades improved. Initially, there will be loneliness in their lives, but most children have a way of bouncing back; it is the adults who have more embedded experiences which require a lot of forgiveness and healing.

Another middle-aged respondent said his teen-age daughter did not like anyone he dated because she wanted him to remarry her mother. The girl allegedly began telling lies on his girlfriend as a way to break them up. He said had he not realized, or learned that she was not telling the truth, that he would have lost his "soul mate."

You must remember the most important factor: "You only have one life." Your son or daughter will have their chance to develop their own lifestyle. Do not set a pattern where the child will seek a situation similar to the one he/she is familiar with because that is what they will choose later in life. Conversely, do not allow your children to prevent you from happiness by trying to control your life. As child psychologists will tell you, all children want their mothers and fathers to be together, no matter what their problems are, and most children want you to stay with an abuser because they do not understand!

As stated throughout this book, if leaving is the only solution, make sure you obtain counseling for the children. School psychologists can assist during this uncomfortable period. Because some children believe they are responsible for their parents' unhappiness, it is very important that they see the parents interacting responsibly during and following the separation. This gives them permission to do the same. If a child sees a parent suffering, the child thinks suffering is what life is about, and, as research has shown, when these children become adults they become the caretakers, nurturers, co-dependents: people who choose to suffer because of other people's problems! If they see a parent abusing, they will believe it is the right way to live.

To reiterate, should you decide to leave an abusive situation, make certain that you are the one making the decision. Do not leave because a lover, friend, or family member says you should. Separating is difficult enough without other outside influences. There might be some very stressful times, and because some children will blame you for the rest of their lives, you want the decision to be totally yours. For example, about 1/4 of the adults I interviewed are still blaming their parents for breaking up, however, about the same number still have questions as to why their mother or father stayed in the abusive relationship! So you see the importance of making a wise choice because no matter what you do, some children will blame you!

There are some adults who grew up in broken homes who confirm Dr. Whitfield's premise: they will not allow themselves to become involved in a serious relationship because they do not trust. Many adults suffer from guilt, shame, and blame because they did not have any counseling following the break-up, and some mothers and fathers are still suffering. Therapy will help you to understand and to be able to work through the hurt, but there are some children and adults, even with therapy, which never seem to function properly after the parents separate. (Research reports this year has proven that many adults from divorced parents still have problems).

It is also reported that some children from disrupted families have a harder time achieving intimacy in relationships or in holding steady jobs, however, some people disagree with this consensus because there are many people who were raised in dysfunctional homes who are very happy, reponsible, and successful people. For example, many of our most successful people were raised by a single mother, a grandmother, etc. Approximately 50% of the respondents were from broken homes, and 20% had never met their father. (The group was ages 40-65. I believe this number is much greater in the age groups 40 and under).

My younger son was too young to remember the abuse; I believe that is why he did well in school, was able to survive the Armed Forces for eight years in Korea, Germany, and throughout the United States, and received several honors as well as completing college courses while enlisted. The other two children (ages 3 and 5) had more problems because they probably remembered, even at that age. Although they were very popular in school and have outgoing personalities, they received more of the "ravages" of his abuse. They were not physically or sexually abused, but they were old enough to understand and hear the arguments, and to realize that his personality would change from time-to-time. The eldest suffered from a bout of drug addiction and both had problems sustaining long-term relationships. On several occasions they acted abusively by pushing or slapping a female as a way to settle conflict; they followed the cycle which some researchers have said occurs when children see dysfunction in a family. It also "bears out" what research has proven: children who are in healthy family relationships are the most adjusted and the most successful. (We are not stating that abused children or those from dysfunctional homes do not succeed). As mentioned earlier, whether a child is affected or not depends on many factors: the individual, the severity of the abuse, whether someone else comes into the child's live and provides love, and if counseling is received.

      It is very important that you alleviate the abuse from a child's life as soon as it shows its face. If the abuser does not get help, then you must remove the children, even if it means going to a shelter. Even though I did remove my sons from the abusive situation, I was not aware that they needed counseling after the demise of the relationship. In retrospect, I believe this caused them to also follow some of his patterns!

      Leaving, when there are children involved, versus protecting you and them from harm, is a very sensitive issue; it is complicated because the choice you make could have a lifelong effect on you, and in some cases, other family members who might have to help or rear the children. If children are neglected, sometimes it is so traumatic that it is difficult to obtain their love and trust again. If you have given your children and yourself the best you have to give, ultimately you will be able to justify whatever decision you make. Most of all do not continue to live in the past or "beat yourself up" because you left. Realize that you did what you thought was best at the time in order to protect them and you. For example, because I did not realize that my sons needed counseling, I did not involve them in therapy. I just tried to be there for them as much as possible and to give them a "well-rounded" lifestyle. (They were also blessed to have my immediate family as a support system!) Even with these things, they probably still suffered. As adults now, they can choose to get help as well as revise the parenting skills that I used and implement new ones for their children.

I must emphasize that this is not a "how-to" book about leaving; instead (as reiterated throughout) it is a book about awareness, power, and choice! It is a sharing tool: a linkage, in an attempt to bring you peace and happiness in your life as well as the lives of your children. If you still believe that leaving the abuser is the only answer, you should develop a "Safety Plan," similar to the one W.O.M.A.N. Inc. has developed as noted via the World Wide Web, May 21, 1997, as follows:

Decide where you will go and how you will get there the next time the person becomes violent. DO THIS, even if you don't think there will be a next time.
- Keep all your important documents in one secure place near an exit in your house or in

a safe place outside your home. This includes your driver's license, birth certificate, medical records, credit cards, marriage license, social security cards, etc.
- Have some money in a safe location, including coins to make calls.
- Keep an extra set of car keys and extra clothing hidden outside your house at a safe location.
- Prepare hand luggage, which includes essential personal articles and keep in a safe place.
- If possible, tell someone you can trust about the violence. Try to develop friendships with neighbors. Ask them to call police if they hear any suspicious noises coming from your home.
- Inform a family member, friend, or coworker you trust of your plans, so you can count on their support at the moment of departure.
- Develop a code word with your children, neighbors, and friends, so that they know that you need to get out now.
- Do not try to fight back if the abuser seems to be "building up," especially if that person gets drunks or high on drugs. Instead get out of the house. If you can't leave safely, keep your back towards an open space, not a corner. In an emergency, call 911 to ask the police for transportation to a safe place and to discuss the possibility of an emergency protective order.
- If you are an immigrant or refugee, you should protect yourself and the children

from getting deported. There are certain provisions under the "Violence Against Women Act" to help you. Contact a domestic violence program or an immigration lawyer for assistance.

There are no prescriptions as to how to exit an abusive relationship when you have children; we can only recommend that it is not healthy for then to be reared in and around abuse. Initially, changing your lifestyle might cause a few problems; this is to be expected. In most cases if you are being abused, you are probably living with fear, depressed, and/or just existing anyway!

Don't negate therapy for yourself. Counseling is a "bridge," which will help you to solve logistical problems relative to housing, medical, social, etc., so do not "rule it out." If you are dissatisfied with one social worker, etc., change to another one. Ask for referrals through friends or contact your local American Medical Association for suggestions. Don't hesitate to use this resource, even prior to leaving.

Because violence will continue in our society, the least you can do for yourself is try to eliminate it in your own life. You cannot wait for the government, legal institutions, churches, schools, etc., to make changes; you can take steps to change it. Maresek gives some examples of ways to take care of yourself if you are living with violence: They are as follows:

- Remove yourself from the cause of the harm, and you should not be too proud to ask others for help. Find a safe environment. If it is safe to move in with relatives or friends, do so,

however, if this will endanger those people, you must find other means: a shelter or another safe place.
- Develop a support system. Surround yourself with people whom you can trust: family, friends, church, support groups, etc. Be a friend to others, then when you need a friend, you will have one. Do not isolate yourself; there is strength in numbers. Sometimes abusers are less likely to confront you if you are not alone.
- Stay healthy - Most of all take care of yourself so that you can handle those important things that you will need to do. Get rest, take walks, and be good to yourself so that you can help your children.
- Regain your sense of humor - Laughter is better medicine than any pills a doctor can prescribe, according to Marecek. Choose friends who can laugh at and with you. Look for movies and television shows that are funny. Seek out people who have good healthy attitudes, because they will bring out the best in you. You will start to feel better once you start laughing. Tragedy can have a humorous side, says Marecek; try it!

W.O.M.A.N., Inc. says, "Remember: You do not deserve to be hit! Once you realize that you are the only person who is responsible for your happiness, you must trust and be sincere in alleviating abuse from your life. You must not worry about the "how-to's" or outcomes; just be clear that abuse is not what you want in your life. You will begin to see changes happening, answers to questions, and you will wonder why you remained so long. Most of all take time to heal and do not be too embarrassed to continually ask others for support.

PART V

HEALING AND RECOVERY

OVERCOMING ABUSE

Practicing Forgiveness. The most important thing that I can say about healing or surviving abuse is that you must forgive the abuser in order to move on! There are people who have committed incidents so horrific that some people have difficulty forgiving, and from my research, approximately 1/3 said they were still unforgiving. Rather than living with past abuse, it is imperative that you seek therapy so that you do not "dwell" on the situation for the remainder of your life. Remember you do not have to forget in order to forgive, but in order to receive your healing and overcome, you must forgive the perpetrator.

Choosing a Therapist. As stated earlier, hypnosis is one way of making contact with your "true" self, according to Marilyn Gordon, author of Healing is Remembering Who You Are: A Guide for Healing Your Mind, Your Emotions, and Your Life. She shares a story of one of her patients, an adult female, who was suffering from severe stomachaches. Under hypnosis, she said she saw children in the schoolyard rejecting her because she was different, and believed she was being rejected by her boyfriend. After the therapist informed her that she was not unworthy, and after the woman revealed other information, the pains in her stomach stopped. She was able to get rid of old "tapes;" negatives which kept her in bondage. Many abusers function as a result of hurting messages other people have given them, and many grow up without getting help. Some believe people have preconceived notions about them, so they either withdraw, become defensive, or abuse others both mentally and physically.

Once you find a therapist with whom you are satisfied, do not be too embarrassed to tell the truth. It is up to the therapist to be an active listener and to tell you what he/she has heard you say. You are there for your own healing and to receive some understanding of what happened, not to point fingers or establish who caused the problems. Stay in therapy as long as you need to. It is imperative that you not leave until you have received adequate help. Remember therapists are there to help, not judge or condemn you. Your story will not shock them, nor will it be too different from anyone else's. So share your true feelings. To reiterate, do seek help if you believe that you are being violated emotionally, physically, or sexually. If someone's actions are causing you prolonged stress; eventually you will get sick.

Be careful in selecting a therapist because there are reports of malpractice. For example, a 34-year old female said her therapist convinced her that her father, a minister, impregnated her and had sexually abused her from age seven until age 14. The father lost his church, job, etc., and the woman later admitted that her therapist convinced her that she had been abused. Not to denigrate therapists' techniques because many people have been helped who had previously hid the memories in order to survive because it was so painful. Once it is "regurgitated" (brought to the surface) most people are able to go on living normal lives.

When seeking a therapist, it is important that you

get references either from an associate or the American Medical Association.

Finding a Spiritual Base. Religion has always, and will always be, a very sensitive issue to discuss. It is very important, however, that you deal with this topic by sharing your beliefs if you are thinking about getting involved with someone, because there are more divorces than ever (and that also applies to people who worship together, separately, or not at all!) It has created a lot of chaos because sometimes differences cannot be resolved, however, there are couples who have been together many years because they have either "merged" their philosophies or agreed to disagree on this topic.

It would certainly add to the relationship if the old adage; "People who pray together stay together" worked for all couples, especially when there are children, but I am sad to report that more than 50% of all marriages end in divorce! There are other statistics that report this number to be more like 60-40 (with the lowest being the ones who remain together!)

Do not be dishonest to a potential mate by saying you will go to church or participate in the religious beliefs in order to further the relationship. Conversely, do not assume another person will get involved in your religion because they say "I love you," or you marry without discussing it. Some people have joined another person's religion with ulterior motives in mind, others will visit a church just to find a mate, and there are those who will attend until you become involved, then they will discontinue!

You must be careful that you are not inviting an abuser into your life by persuading him/her to worship with you or believe that everyone who attends church is honorable. There are abusers in all walks of life! For example, a friend's daughter who had never been married was supposed to have a great job, home, etc. She was allegedly bilked of home, retirement, and bank account after meeting a man who represented himself as a minister whose wife had passed. Because he was supposed to have a church in another town, he traveled weekly between both places. Shortly after they married, she died of cancer. When the family contested the Will, they learned that she had, in fact, signed everything over to him! They also learned that he had taken several other women the same way, always representing himself as a minister!

    Having the same religious beliefs can certainly help in a relationship, but the bottom line is that a good relation- ship is based on love, respect, integrity, and communication. People who do not have these concepts in the relationship will have problems no matter what their beliefs are! Some marriages, believe it or not, have worked when the beliefs are different because they include the above-mentioned factors. For example, my godmother and husband are of different beliefs and have been happily married 48 years; he is Baptist, and she is non-denominational. Another of my best friends is Baptist, and her husband never went to church but had a belief in God. They were married 43 years before he died. There are also other couples who have successful relationships, and they do not belong to a formal religion. Their marriages are successful because they implement good concepts into their lives. They do not violate each other, are socially concerned about what happens in the world, and they give of their time and money to help the less fortunate. In other words, these relationships are made up of two loving and respectful people who are practicing the "Golden Rule," to treat others as they would treat themselves! Some people might say, "That is not enough, they are not a part of any religion." Not to denigrate anyone because I am a devout Christian, but I must admit that many of the religious couples are also part of the 50% that are divorcing!

Because of this depressing statistics, some churches are now working (especially in America) specifically to reduce this divorce rate, according to Michael J. McManus, author of Helping Your Friends and Family Avoid Divorce, Become a Marriage Saver. He believes that people should avoid marriage if there are problems in the beginning! It is also his opinion that you should not live together prior to marriage. In fact, the National Survey of Families and Households found that in 1989 there was a 50% higher rate of divorce or separation for those couples who lived together prior to marriage versus the ones who married without cohabiting. McManus says it is sad that people who do live together, marry, and divorce, do not learn a lesson; they move on to do the same thing with other partners!

Mr. and Mrs. McNamus' conduct weekend encounters where couples are taught new ways to love each other. After attending, some have decided their problems are just too overwhelming and agree to a peaceful divorce. According to the McManus', 40,000 of the 50,000 couples in Canada and the United States saved their marriages as a result of this seminar. They travel the country encouraging pastors of churches to use the community marriage covenants. As of November 1996 forty-three cities had adopted it. Many churches are now incorporating pre-marriage counseling programs for couples contemplating marriage, as well as seminars and retreats for married couples.

To reiterate, religion can play a very important role in keeping couples together if the relationship is built on love as well as good communication. I must admit, my ex-husbands and I never discussed religion prior to our marriages, but I was naive' enough to believe that once we got married, they would occasionally visit my church, even if they did not join. Not to say that their attending would have changed anything; but maybe the first one would not have been physically abusive, and the second one, who was emotionally abusive, would have been honest with me prior to asking for a divorce.

Another alarming problem some respondents alluded to, is that when their spouse joined a church or practiced a religious or spiritual concept (and they did not) they were no longer compatible. In other words, what they had in common was no longer relevant. For example, a male respondent said; "After I started attending church, I did not have a desire for alcohol, yet my wife still wanted to go to bars. Eventually this separation lead to our divorce." Another response was: "Before I joined church, my husband and I seemed to have more in common, however, the interests we had with other couples no longer existed. We started going our separate ways, and eventually he found someone else."

Another respondent said he was referred to as a "sinner" because he did not want to attend the wife's church. He said the relationship ended because he felt he was doing something wrong if he had sex with her. In another situation, the female became a minister, and the relationship ended immediately. I found that response very interesting because most females stay with their husbands when they become ministers. Of interest is that most females changed their religious practices to the males, would visit with him, etc., but fewer males were willing to leave theirs for the spouses, and many were unwilling to even visit!

Because I have no factual information or statistics on the percentage of people whose relationships work when they have different beliefs, I can only state that sometimes relationships end when basic interests are not the same. (This is a paradox because research has proven that people do divorce even when they have shared interests). I am not stating that people do not change, because some of them do. I am only reiterating that both people should be very clear, honest, and flexible in dealing with the subject of religion. If you believe you are compatible in other areas, and your only problem is the differences in your religious beliefs or practices, you might want to seek counseling in an attempt to save the relationship, especially if you are happy.

Many people are now reporting that they find spiritual fulfillment from various means. For example, some respondents said they do not practice a formal religion; instead, they incorporate meditation, yoga, music, writing poetry, jogging, etc., which some people believe is not enough. Personally, I prefer to incorporate all of those as well as to have a personal relationship with a "higher being" that I refer to as God, however, I do not believe that I should violate another human being because he/she believes differently! Many people abuse others when they do not believe like they do. We must be very careful that we not violate another person's rights - and that also means the right to choose what they believe in!

Kivel provides a very interesting and controversial theory when he says abusers do not have a spiritual life (connection to a force greater than theirs). It is his opinion that these people do not respect others, some believe they are in charge of everything here on earth, and many turn to drugs, violence, etc., due to the "emptiness" they feel. Conversely, some people become so dependent on spirituality that they start believing in their leaders; in other words, they worship a human being! It is not wise to give your powers to a leader or an organization. Most of you will remember the Heavens' Gates people who decided to kill themselves because the leader made the decision that they should all drink poison and take a spaceship to heaven. They were all victims of another person's insanity. That is not the only case. The most famous was Jim Jones who also had hundreds of people drink a poisonous solution, which killed them.

Other sick parents have beaten and killed their children in the name of religion because of their misunderstanding or someone else's interpretation. There are many sick people who represent themselves as religious leaders, so you must have a discerning mind so that you think for yourself as well as be able to delineate what another human being is saying! For example, some religious organizations use abusive tactics by saying the Bible states men should be heads of the household. Maybe this was true years ago when: men were in the home, women stayed home and raised the children, and marriages did not end in divorce. In my opinion, this is an antiquated belief because in many homes, the male is missing or does not have a job, secondly, some males believe if women do not "obey" them, they are treated abusively. Finally, many women run organizations, have businesses, and are in powerful roles just as men are, and many believe decisions should be jointly made or made alone! Some men - not all - have used this to take advantage of their spouse.

      In summary, whether you are religious or spiritual, etc., (the term which many people are now using) you should always use your intelligence, wise judgment, etc., to determine if the act is a violation of your right to be a secure and healthy individual! Approximately 75% of the respondents said it was a requirement that their mate have a belief in God, but 50% said it was a requirement that they attend the same church or have the same belief.

Learning to Love You. You deserve to be loved. Some people believe they have done something to cause themselves to be violated. In my own case, both times I searched for answers and constantly revised what I was doing in order to please the perpetrators. What I did not understand at the time was that, you cannot please an abuser! Some people, after living in an abusive environment, believe they are not entitled to happiness. I wanted to stop whatever was causing my ex-husband's anger, however, after learning there was nothing I could do that would make a change, I decided to leave! What I did not realize at the time was, he had not forgiven his father for the alleged abuses that were rendered to him and was still living with the pain. Because he did not understand how the cycle of violence works (he did not have counseling) it was impossible for him to share love with anyone else.

Meditating. Another way to make contact with the "real" self, alleviate stress, and continually be peaceful is through meditation. You must learn to let go of the negative thoughts and discomforts of anything that does not give love to you. First, relax and let go of any stresses. Take a deep breath and exhale. Repeat this many times throughout the day, allowing your body to relax totally. You should feel an inner joy that you can obtain at any time you so desire. If you will practice this daily, you will notice that you will begin to feel better. As you practice this breathing and relaxing process, you can operate from this place in your life. The more you do this, the more relaxed you will become until you find yourself (in most situations) always peaceful! You will be more in control of emotions.

Some people perform this exercise at work to alleviate tension, but you are free to get in touch with your "higher" self whenever you feel the need. Eventually, after incorporating this into your life, you will be able to function from a peaceful state of mind no matter what happens. You owe this to your mind and body!

Using Affirmations. We have discussed the use of affirmations previously in regards to stress in the workplace; however, they can be used for many reasons. For example, when I was writing my thesis, because I divorced during the time, I had to stop the writing and move out of my comfortable home. It was very difficult to get started again, so I used positive verses and affirmation to keep me going. I posted them in my bathroom, bedroom, on the refrigerator, and in my purse, etc. When I would become stressed, or a crisis occurred, I would go from room-to-room reciting them. When I was not at home, I would open my wallet and repeat various ones many times until I could truly feel and believe what they were saying.

Marianne Williamson, author of <u>A Woman's Worth</u>, also agrees with other experts regarding using positive verse for reinforcement. It is her opinion that you should repeat one at least ten times, believe what you are saying, (simply repeating it does not help) and your life should change as a result. Whatever mechanism you choose, you should understand that you are not the abused child or hurt personality anymore. (If you are the abuser, use this verses also). You no longer have to carry the burden of someone else's violations.

<u>Analyzing the Self</u>. Once you recognize that you are living with an abuser, whether you leave or not, you should do a self-evaluation. Try to determine what it is that is keeping you there, why you are allowing the abuse, and what you are getting from the relationship. Review your own faults as well as your successes. One way to do this is to write them down. This process is very therapeutic, and you can read it over-and-over to determine where you need to improve. Make a list of what makes you feel unhappy or uncomfortable. Review the past, the good memories and bad, accomplishments, hurts, as well as the times you hurt someone. Write about relationships and family. This might be time-consuming, and some things will be very painful.

You can separate the sections by family, jobs, relationships (male and female) etc., to determine if you see a pattern. In most cases, you will. For example, one respondent said she wondered why all of her male relationships were alcoholics, and after entering therapy, it was determined that she met them in bars! The therapist explained that her pattern of meeting men was to go where people drank, consequently, those were the men she was involved with. The woman had not realized this, but after reviewing her past, she realized that she was not consciously looking for men who drank, she was only going to bars because she enjoyed dancing. She began exploring other social activities, for example, she started taking golfing lessons and after nine months received a marriage proposal.

When you are unhappy, you must stop to analyze your situation to determine how you might change it. Most people, rather than searching themselves, would rather blame the other person or conditions for their problems. Sometimes another person is creating the negativity in your life, but if you are allowing it to continue by not asking yourself why, you are just as guilty. Many people make excuses rather than making changes. Most people are always ready to fix others, but they spend less time on themselves! The answers are there, but you must listen as well as be truthful to yourself. Once you have designated what your problems are as well as your self-worth, you should not continue to blame others, because you are free.

If there are things in your life that are not fulfilling, you have the power to change them. This also means you might have to depend on yourself for finances, emotional support, or anything else. If you want a career or change of career, you should either take classes, special training, or attend seminars that will lead you to your goal. When you stop depending on others, you will find that life does not end! Most of all, you will find that no one else has to change in order for you to feel good! An example of this was emphasized by Mr. Nelson Mandela, ANC President and South African activist, who was jailed for over 20 years, on <u>The Oprah Winfrey Show</u> (November 27, 2000). When she asked him, "How do you bring peace to a chaotic situation or country?" He replied, "By being humble, but first taking time for self-discovery!" He said incarceration allowed him to take the time to do this. He did not allow the so-called negative experience to deteriorate him. Instead, he used the time to read, write, meditate, etc., in order to preserve his powers. Consequently, he has forgiven the system and is not a bitter person! Many people are not as fortunate as Mr. Mandela. He has forgiven the South African government and others and did not allow them to imprison his mind. As a result, he is a much happier person. You can become a much happier person if you take the time to incorporate some of the above-referenced concepts into your life.

PART VI

SUMMARY

WHAT CAN SOCIETY DO TO PREVENT VIOLENCE?

Society has to work together to get rid of the violence in all areas. To do this, we must all participate in the following:

    1) Change patriarchal and sexist practices
    2) Promote respect for all family members and others
    3) Educate and sensitize the media so they do not encourage domestic violence
    4) Develop more programs to teach children meanings of abuse and the tactics for handling various types of abuse
    5) Present legislation to lawmakers at all levels to change laws of abusers: longer incarceration, more rehabilitation facilities (not jails) stricter training, counseling, and follow-up programs, and more shelters for both men and women
    6) Train health care workers, social workers, police, and teachers to recognize and report abuse. (Ranked the most important of proposed solutions by U. S. Advisory Board on Child Abuse and Neglect's Panel, AmericaOnline, November 7, 1996, who recommended tougher laws for prosecuting people who abuse kids and more abuse-prevention programs). One of the main purposes of this book is to train those in authority (including parents) as well as to teach others how to recognize and overcome abuse.

Child Abuse. To protect children from sexual abuse we must change the attitude that children are property of parents. We must dispel myths of abuse, which hopefully I have done in this book; and more treatment programs must be made available for men, women, and families. Funding must be allocated from all sources: Federal, State, County, churches, corporations, etc., because abuse affects everyone. If you or a member of your family have not been a victim of incest, sexual abuse, rape, domestic violence, or workplace harassment, if you allow pedophiles, other family members, people in sports or other higher profile arenas to continue abusing, you are contributing by allowing it in your community!

Children should not be returned to the custody of abusive parents. Many abusive spouses continue to receive custody of the children, although experts agree that spousal abuse is one of the leading indicators of child abuse and neglect. According to Congressional Caucus for Women's Issues, Inform's Report of January 14, 1997, only ten states and the District of Columbia are the only states with laws saying children should not return to abusive parents. We need more states to implement this legislation. When violators harm others, some of those victims then seek their prey. When they multiply, they need others to attack; hopefully it won't be you or me! Get involved; accept Cooney's challenged, as noted previously.

Report abuse. If you know someone who is being victimized, who has not reported it, encourage that person to do so. We all know that it is impossible to save an entire society, and I am not advocating that we can, however, you can start somewhere. Begin with yourself by not allowing it into your life; then educate and share with your family and friends. Inform victims and report abusers. (If it is safely possible.) If you know that someone in your family is being abusive to another person, you should:

1) Call it to their attention immediately. If it is another adult within your household, you should let them know what they are doing is wrong.

2) If a friend or family member is a victim and believes there are no answers, refer them to this text as well as the other resources mentioned in the Resources and Bibliography. Refer them to an organization. (See organizational list.)

3) If there are victims who are children, or children who are "bullies," report it. If it is the teacher, children should tell another teacher, counselor, or administrator.

4) Be careful and do make wise choices when you report abuse. It might sound like I'm again "talking from both sides of my mouth," but I am not. There are times when you can safely report abuse by just going to a telephone and reporting it, however, there are definite occasions when you will be killed if you get involved. For example, telephoning Child Protective Services to report someone who is beating a child you have personally seen battered and bruised, or calling 911 if you see someone being beaten on the street, is not too much to ask. In fact, California Governor Gray Davis signed a bill in September 2000 making it a crime for anyone who has knowledge of a sexual or violent act on a child under the age of 14. Violators may be convicted of a misdemeanor and could serve six months in county jail. This Law, the Sherrice Iverson Child Victim Protection Act, was inspired

following the rape and strangulation of a seven-year old girl by a 19-year old man in a Las Vegas casino in 1997 (as reported by Las Vegas Review Journal (9/10/98). It is named after the victim and was first presented by Democratic Representative Nick Lampson. Democratic Senator Barbara Boxer (California) further implemented the Bill to indicate that States would be subject to losing Federal funding if they do not pass it by December 31, 2004!

  5) Should you see a woman or man being beaten or robbed on the streets, if it is humanly possible that you can enter a business or residence, you should report it. I am not saying that you should involve yourself in a shoot-out, or physically get involved with a man and woman fighting; but certainly you can call the police! As a citizen, voter, etc., if you believe you have the right to vote "ugly" politicians out of office, you are also responsible for incarcerating "ugly" abusers!

  Many people are being responsible citizens. For example in 1997 in Los Angeles, Children's Hospital unveiled a bright blue sculpture showing the silhouettes of children on top of large toy blocks entitled "Stolen Lives." It represented 17 children ages newborn to age four who were killed by a parent or caretaker. Gil Garcetti (District Attorney at the time) said with voice cracking, "Children are dying at home, and their lives are stolen by people who are supposed to be loving and protecting." The inscriptions on each figure showed their horrible deaths: some kicked, punched, and repeatedly beaten, and according to <u>The Oakland Tribune</u>, April 26, 1997, one died at birth, suffocating in the bucket of feces into which he was born! The sculpture is a reminder to urge people to report child abuse before it escalates.

Many children do not report abuse because they feel intimidated when being questioned by so many people. Some, after being questioned, will even deny that it ever occurred. In California, Alameda County is trying to alleviate this by opening a facility called the Child Abuse Listening Interviewing and Coordination Center in San Leandro. There are a number of these centers in California developed to cut down on the number of people who interview the victim. Alameda County's facility is funded partly by a state grant from the Department of Social Services; however, it must also rely on public and private donations or grants, according to Lisa Dobey, Director. Opening in April 1998, they consolidated the interviews usually conducted separately by police, district attorneys, defense lawyers, and social service agencies. Hopefully, this will lessen the trauma that some young assault victims undergo as well as to prevent so many children from dying. This is a very positive venture that many counties should develop.

Confidentiality is another problem the courts have to deal with. Tara Aronson wrote an article entitled "Who Will Save the Children," that deals with legal professionals of Santa Clara County's juvenile system. She said society must help raise other children as they do their own children. She cited 1,300 children who died in 1993 while in the parents' care. She told about a four-year old whose mother was a mentally disturbed 18-year old, who saw her father's bloody suicide attempt at the age of four. She is alleged to have locked her daughter in the closet, beat her with high heels and coat hangers, and put salt in her mouth to keep her from crying! The judge requested that the child be returned to this mother, because she said she was not using drugs! John Hubner and Jill Wolfson authors of <u>Somebody Else's Children</u>, according to Aronson, asked the question: "Should we be risking the lives of children by leaving them with dead-end, dangerous families?" They admit there is no one policy or solution to answer these problems. My question to society is: "At what point is a child considered abused enough? If I would answer my own question, I would respond, "When he or she is dead!"

    Fathers are now taking active roles in parenting, as stated previously. They are doing the work which mothers have always done! In fact, many are raising children alone, and some are staying at home while the mother works. One divorced male respondent admitted it was not easy to be the "mom," that he now has more respect for women. Another stated he gets "backlash" at work from the other men and his employers when he shared that he is taking an active role in parenting. He said he does not receive promotions, is made fun of by other males, and is not considered a team player. Supervisors "frown" on it because he has to take his vacation and other time off to be with the children, but says he would not trade it for anything!

    Tom Brokaw, <u>NBC</u> News Reporter, (April 23, 1998) quoted a study conducted by Loyola University that confirmed what the above gentleman is saying. According to the study, more men are revising their work schedules to take more active roles in children's lives; however, they make 20% less than the "go-getters" are making and do not "go up the corporate ladder!" The important factor from this report is that children of these fathers are twice as likely to get A's! It is shocking to learn that employers are not sensitive to these dedicated men. Many men's organizations are now teaching effective co-parenting, because some say they want to share, and others are against women being the sole decision maker.

There are many others working towards promoting and supporting fatherhood and men's roles in families, for example, The Bay Area Father Involvement and Male Responsibility Initiative kicked off its campaign by holding a one-day conference in Oakland in June 1997. Workshops were held on "Cycle of Violence," "Female Roles and Obstacles to Involving Fathers in Families, " and "Male Rites of Passage." The conference was co-sponsored by Oakland Healthy Start, who is working to teach fathers to share a leadership role in child rearing as a co-parent. More information is available on the Internet site at FatherNet or by calling (800) 852-8112. They are doing an excellent job of working with the entire family.

Another group that is doing a wonderful job is the National Center for Fathering in Kansas City, Missouri, founded by Ken R. Canfield. The group has developed a fathering training program for individual dads as well as for groups up to 1,000 or more. Canfield researched the practices and attitudes of over 5,000 fathers across the nation and identified 300 who were considered most effective. He then delineated seven differences between the two groups and shares those tips and secrets in a resource book entitled The 7 Secrets of Effective Fathers, which distinguishes effective fathers from those who are considered average. (It is also available in audiotape). They also provide seminars for men, women, and fathers-only groups.

Gavin de Becker, a security consultant, is

another resourceful person working on alleviating violence. He has written a book entitled, <u>The Gift of Fear</u>, which discusses way to predict violence through human intuition: the gut feeling that tells you that you are in danger, as reported in <u>Parade Magazine</u> (May 18, 1997). Becker has used his program to assess threats to governors, members of Congress, and Supreme Court Justices. He developed MOSAIC-50, which focuses on abused children who are at risk and will provide this system to people through the <u>World Wide Web</u>. We applaud Mr. Becker for implementing both programs that will definitely help in decreasing violence of children and women.

Domestic Violence. A report from the National Institute of Mental Health, November 16, 1996, reveals prevention will have to start with people changing their attitudes toward violence and women. The tolerance of family violence as a way of life in one generation encourages family violence in another generation. Because abusers do not learn to deal with anger as a child, they handle their frustrations through aggression. They should learn that it is human to feel anger but inhuman to release those feelings by abusing others, says NIMH. They must learn how to deal with their emotions through acceptable behavior, thereby gaining respect for themselves and others.

The Federal Government has a few programs to assist states in helping female violence victims, as reported by Congressional Caucus for Women's Issues (<u>wwwInform Editor</u>, January 14, 1997. They are as follows:

1) Family Violence Prevention and Services

Act of 1984, administered by the Department of Health and Human Services. They provide grants to states to establish, maintain, and expand shelters, and other programs: child care programs, counseling, and related services to domestic violence victims and their dependents. They also allocate funds for training and technical assistance to law enforcement agencies, authorizes a National Clearinghouse on Family Violence Prevention, and provides grants for family violence research and other related activities. Eight-five percent of the money is used for state-run domestic violence programs, and 60% of this goes to shelter-related assistance.

  2) Victims of Crime Act (VOCA). They authorize four programs to assist crime victims. The first provides funds to crime victim assistance programs, including rape crisis programs and battered women's shelters as well as law enforcement-based crisis intervention. Over 44% of the funds go to these programs. The second portion of this program reimburses mental health counseling, medical expenses, lost wages, and funeral expenses; about 45% of the funds are used for this. The Federal Government reimburses states for up to 40% of what they spend on crime victim compensation programs. The other two programs are considerably smaller: one provides funds to assist victims of crimes committed on federal property such as prisons, and the other assists child abuse and child sexual abuse programs through the Children's Justice Act.

  3) The Office for Victims of Crime (OVC) established by the Justice Department in 1983 supports training programs for law enforcement officers, prosecutors, the clergy, medical, mental

health, and victim assistance professionals; all of whom come in contact with victims of crime.

4) The Omnibus Crime Control Act of 1990 deals with colleges and universities disclosing to students the number of serious crimes: rape, murder, and robbery, involving students on or near campus. Convicted sex offenders must undergo AIDS testing, and sexual assault victims receive counseling supported through these funds. This program began in 1992.

5) Immigration Reform for Battered Spouses deals with foreigners married to American citizens. Prior to 1990 foreigners could not leave an abuser without risk of being deported if they had not been in the United States two years. This enactment waives the two-year period.

6) Sense of Congress Resolution on Domestic Violence, passed in 1990, says it is detrimental to the child to be placed in the custody of an abusive parent.

In many large cities, communities are working with schools to alleviate domestic violence. For example, in Oakland, California (December 1997) the Oakland Domestic Violence Prevention Collaborative, composed of seven agencies, interviewed 50 students on their impressions of domestic violence. An eight-grade student designed a billboard on domestic violence, and her design, along with two others, is one of 15 placed next to schools to sway students from entering into or tolerating abusive relationships. Hopefully students will know about domestic violence and will be able to discuss it with their parents, other family members, and friends. Many districts have incorporated conflict management programs into their curriculum.

Many hospitals are becoming involved, because so many women and men are now appearing in emergency rooms as a result of sexual abuse and domestic violence. Most recently, Kaiser Permanente, in conjunction with the University of California, San Francisco, sponsored a treatment and research program for women who had been sexually assaulted. They offered evaluation and medication treatment to help relieve symptoms of nightmares, anxiety, depression, anger, and emotional numbing.

Discontinuance of funding for programs working to stop violence has become a real problem in recent years. One very viable program faced with this is Domestic Violence Response Team (DVRT) who trains nurses, social workers, doctors, and medical aides at 12 Alameda County hospitals to pay close attention to women's symptoms. Because 30% of women entering the hospital suffer from domestic battery injuries, some medical professionals are now trained to recognize women when they say they have a headache, but are actually beaten or shaken by a partner. They train medical personnel to ask particular questions to ascertain whether ailments and injuries are caused by domestic violence. Those who admit to needing help are referred to county domestic-violence agencies that receive state funding. These grants are now targeted for discontinuance, even though they have helped many women who would not have been reached otherwise. Hopefully there will be reconsideration of the necessity for these grants.

Parenting Teens. Kivel, cited previously, believes that society discriminates against teens who are faced with surmountable problems: drugs, AIDS, unemployment, and abuse, etc., and some are uninformed about sex. Many abused teens do not succeed following sexual, physical, emotional, or drug abuse. Some withdraw or blame themselves for the abuse. Teen suicide is on the rise, because many teens feel powerless. If they are gay, lesbian, poor, a person of color, etc., they are faced with more abuse, and Black and Latino teens are more apt to face discipline problems, suspension and arrests, according to Kivel.

    Adults must help teens build the power to protect themselves to make meaningful choices. Adults must take time to listen to what teens are saying and must be their allies. If you are a parent, try to remember when you were a teen. Think about all of the problems you dealt with and how powerless you felt. Most people will agree that the problems that we believed were overwhelming are not as bad as the ones the teens are faced with since the 90's. For example, as a teen-ager, I only went to two youngsters' funerals, and that was traumatic for me. Ask any 15 to 19-year old how many of their family members, friends, or associates have died. You will be shocked! (In 1998 two 14 and 15-year old girls died at school: one while playing soccer and the other participating in physical education. Allegedly they died of heart attacks. Many children are now going to funerals because of friends who were killed at school).

    The problems for children and teens are so overwhelming, first of all, because nothing is sacred anymore! For example, the children and teens are faced with situations that we never knew as an adult. Television talk shows, some of which are informational, leave nothing to the imagination.

They allow guests to use vulgar language, discuss what they do sexually, fight, etc., in other words, children and teens see other people acting outrageous, so some of them believe that in order to be popular, they have to live a similar lifestyle.

The Playboy channels on television show people performing all types of sexual acts: group, oral, gay/lesbian, etc., and these videos can also be purchased. Because some teens are already being abused, their self-esteem is not being reinforced with positive messages. Consequently those teens trying to live so-called "normal lives" are sometimes viewed as "square," and that causes another problem for the parents. What most people do not understand is that peer pressure is much greater than parental pressures! Because children want to be accepted, especially by their friends, they listen to them and ignore their parents' teachings! Trying to keep your teen sane during these periods is the "64,000 question!" I understand and sympathize with the parents who have teens as well as those rearing young children, because my sons graduated in 1980 and '82, and it was very difficult for me. Although I had certain rules, other youngsters were influencing them to do things that were not in accordance with what I had taught.

For solutions, I can only suggest that you continually discuss the issues with others through attending parenting meetings, seeking counseling for yourself and your teen, and talking with your minister (if you attend a church), as well as the school counselors and psychologists. Do not give up - even though it might seem that once you solve one problem, another evolves! One story that a woman shared with me, which was quite depressing, involved her 14-year old girl. She said she and her husband felt they could never leave home because their daughter was always getting in trouble or "seeking something to do that was wrong." She said they never took a vacation (not even for a few days) because they could not relax knowing she was getting in trouble. That is a sad way to live, and it also causes stress, high blood pressure, and heart attacks.

As parents, you must find some free time for yourself. You cannot give your life totally to another person; that is a form of abuse. Finding balance in your life with a problematic teen-ager is a challenge, however, should you not allow that person to control your life. I am sad to report that some parents have had to resort to finding a teen group home or other form of institution for their child. Some parents do not look for the available resources because of an unruly teen and will wait until the teen is incarcerated. In most occasions, it is too late to take the necessary steps.

For those of you who do not have children or a family, there are people at school, your job, church who might need your assistance. You do not have to go too far to know that society needs help with its youngsters! Volunteer some of your time and give advice which you would use for yourself, but try to be as objective as possible. Many people are hesitant about becoming involved, but Kivel says we are already involved - and he is absolutely correct! Most of us live in fear because violence exists in our neighborhoods.

Kivel says no one can tell you how to confront a violent man, but we must let these abusers know we do not support them! For example, males in sports and other prominent actors should not be held in high esteem when they are abusive.

They should be treated just as other abusers, that is, to undergo therapy and/or incarceration.

PART VII

RECLAIMING YOUR BIRTHRIGHT

TESTIMONIES OF SURVIVORS

Recognize Abuse for What It Is. Separate the love issue, forgive and forget (if you can) but most of all, you have got to move on physically and mentally from the negative occurrence. Constant reliving it will only make you ill. It is nothing wrong with recounting it during counseling or therapy to bring it to the surface of your memory (as has been repeated throughout this book) however, if you are constantly holding it in the conscious mind, it will prevent you from becoming involved in other positive endeavors. I challenge you to forgive as the following people have.

Recognizing abuse is similar to the anecdote about recognizing a snake. When you are ill - you can't recognize a snake. In recovery - you see a snake, know it's a snake, but still play with it. After recovery (once you are healed) you see a snake, know it's a snake but cross over to the other side of the road! So when you recognize abuse, make a move, even if it is only to tell someone or to ask for the name of a good therapist.

It was overwhelming to learn, during the research phase, how many people have overcome. In fact, some of the details were so gruesome that it was difficult for me to understand how they survived, but they did, I did, and you can!
One of those survivors is Carl Brown, a Bay area poet, who wrote <u>Abuse: From My Mind</u>, a book of poetry about his experiences. He says his mission is to reach at least one person who has been, or is

being, abused, to let them know how they can survive and start a healing process that will lead to a productive life. One of his verses, which touched my heart, reads as follows: "I survived the game. My Freedom is reclaimed."

To those of you who have survived, you definitely understand what Mr. Brown is saying. To those of you who believe, for some reason, that you have to accept what is happening to you, know there is an answer. If you take one step towards alleviating it, someone will be there with open arms to help you with that next step. You will be surprised as to how many other people are working in your behalf, just as we are. No matter how drastic the situation, you must understand that there are solutions - there is hope.

One of the "hope" stories was reported by Katie Couric, NBC Reporter on the Today Show in 1998. She interviewed a concert pianist who had been sexually and physically abused for many years by her father, a minister. Not only did he abuse her; he also abused his two sons, one of whom committed suicide. The father is alleged to have been so obsessed, he had her tell a lie that her brother had been killed in a car accident, and the obituary and papers reported the lies! The most poignant and "tear-jerking" portion of her story is when she referred to how the janitor saw her in the basement of their home when she was 15 years old following one of the sexual encounters. According to this woman, as she was coming from the basement with sticky hands, the janitor said, "Daddy shouldn't do this to his little girl...Let me wash your hands for you." She said she will never forget his statement, because it was the most touching memory she has. She went on to say how she had been a pianist for many years, however, when she left home, she suddenly lost her memory for seven years. During this time she was hospitalized, attempted suicide, and underwent repressed recovery therapy. She later saw a note written by her father, apparently to excuse what he had done, saying, "Daddy lost family in holocaust." She said apparently this was his way of explaining what he had done to them for many years, but she said she also thought about what she had lost!

    She decided to confront her parents when she was in her mid-30's by writing a letter to her father. He requested that she meet him in a field alone. She said she feared what he might do, so did not go. She discussed the abuse with her mother who denied that it ever happened! This woman has forgiven her parents, but stated she will never be totally recovered because the parents will not tell the truth. She said today she cannot "stand" to hear the keys of a typewriter, because the father used to type his sermons on Saturday nights, and the sound brings back those memories!

    This young woman says the abuse gets imprinted in your body, and although she considers herself well and happily married; she said her recovery does not bring her brothers back, but her belief in God and playing the piano is the way she shows forgiveness! According to Couric, the parents were invited to the interview but refused, and the father wrote Couric a letter saying he did not molest her, but he believes she was.

    This is such a sad story; you would think a minister would want his daughter to be healed by simply telling the truth. Her story is not unique; there are many people living in pain because they are too embarrassed to face the truth. Some people believe the pains will just "go away," but they do not; in most occasions, it only lessens!

Another touching story that occurred on Geraldo's show this year involves an 11-year old girl who confronted her grandfather for the first time after he allegedly abused her for many years. She said each time she would tell her mother, the grandfather would call her a lie, so she was disbelieved. She wrote a letter to Geraldo and appeared with her mother. She spoke with "power" when she said, "All those years you called me a lie. I now know that you did abuse me, and it began the night of my grandmother's funeral!" Everyone in the audience, including the grandfather, was shocked. He did not respond. She went on to tell him that she forgave him, that he was the one with the problem, not her, as she was lead to believe. This young girl is now able to reclaim her birthright qualities! She has dumped the pain, given it back to the person who owned the problems, and has also forgiven him.

The above anecdotes involve lessons in forgiveness, however, it reveals two very important factors: no matter how deep the pain, you can survive. You might be victimized, but you don't have to remain a victim! With continued therapy, reclaiming your self-esteem, etc., as well as making contact with your "inner voice" or "higher self," etc., you can rise above abuse and move on to a life of peace as these survivors have!

YOUR BIRTHRIGHT ENTITLEMENTS

I believe that each person is entitled to certain rights and privileges simply by being born! I call these your "birthright qualities or entitlements:" those innate or inborn powers consisting of love, faith, joy, hope, peace, and more. Many people spend their entire life searching for these gifts, and according to Margaret Young in Cameron's book (referenced earlier) who says people live their lives backwards: they obtain things so they will be happier. She says you must first be who you really are, then do what you need to do, to have what you really want!

Another very powerful motivator, Dorothy Corkill Briggs, author of <u>Celebrate Yourself - Enhancing Your Own Self-Esteem</u>, says the "treasure" you seek lies within that peace and love are already yours. Once you are aware of this power, you know that it is constant, in other words, you cannot obtain it from superficialities: looks, materials, money, degrees, drugs, etc. People who have discovered this peace know that it is the most important asset you can ever obtain! It is priceless, and, from my experience and others, I believe it includes the following concepts.

<u>The Right to Happiness</u>. According to the constitution, each person has the right to "life, liberty, and pursuit of happiness." However you would be surprised as to how many unhappy people there are in this world. Diane Ackerman, contributing author of <u>Parade</u> Magazine, shares a very overwhelming theory in her article, "The Fears That Save Us," when she says Americans rank 12th out of a list of 39 countries on the happiness scale.

Norway, Denmark, Sweden, and Finland are the happiest: countries that have gloomy weather! She attributes it to the fact that most Americans expect happiness, but pursue it superficially. When they no longer have things, most of them believe they have failed and become unhappy!

Barry Neil Kaufman, author of <u>Happiness Is A Choice</u>, also wonders why most people are unhappy. He is an expert on this issue and has worked with people around the United States. He says no matter where people are from, they all have something in common: the desire to be happy, loving, and loved. He makes an excellent point when he says, "If we're so smart, why aren't we happy…We can fly, freeze images on film, use invisible radio waves, and perform laser surgery, just to mention a few; yet we are just as angry as we were when we "fought with stones!" He goes on to quote Abraham Lincoln when he says: "Most folks are about as happy as they make up their minds to be, and no single energy would have as great an impact on the world as that of one truly happy and loving person!"

Kaufman recommends starting with you. He says if you can be happy, then you will allow others that same freedom. Then our offspring will believe happiness is a natural way of life!

The Right to Love. Love means many things to many people, as discussed previously, however, "respect" is at the top of my priority list! I do not believe you can have love without it, and I believe most people are in unhappy relationships because they do not respect themselves, their family members, or others.

If you check most dictionaries, you will note

that respect is not included as a definition for the word "love." The words listed are: affection, attachment, a strong liking, passionate, fond of, devotion, infatuation, sexual passion, or its gratification, etc.

Many people fall in love with the external qualities of a person, not to say that one's appearance is not important, because it is to most of us, but I only emphasize that judging a person solely for looks might cause stress or deception. You could also end up with an abuser by selecting for outward appearances (as discussed previously). Love should be the most important criteria when selecting a mate.

Marilyn Gordon, author of <u>Healing Is Remembering Who You Are</u>, says people are born with an "Inner Core" or "Essence," which she believes is made up of love, wisdom, and strength. Most people's problems stem from not staying in touch with this original state, but we allow experiences, conditioning, and personalities to cover up this "core." She says, "peel off" the layers of experiences and seek your core, which will reveal the love within you. Rather than looking for sweetness in food, closeness in relationships, and a "high" through alcohol or drugs, seek your birthright assets!

Another icon and famous author, Deepak Chopra, M.D., is also in agreement. In his book <u>Ageless Body - Timeless Mind</u>, he says people become confused about whether they are lovable because they are not aware. He says we should live from the level of awareness that says, "I am love," that you should "peel back those layers" of negativity, conflict, and contradiction to discover your basics: love, compassion, beauty, and awareness, and when you can live from this level, you will not allow abuse. You can then affirm: "I am aware, I am love, and I have purpose!"

The Right to Create. Each person has a purpose for being, and many people do not understand this until something happens to shake up their familiar lifestyle, however, some never realize why they are here! It is usually those crises like the death of a family member, friend, job loss, an accident, surgery, and divorce, etc., that makes people "move to higher levels!" This has happened to me on many occasions, and several times I believed I could not go on, yet I survived because I was forced to "reach" for those innate qualities. For example, following the death of my best friend, as discussed earlier, during the time that I was grieving, for some strange reason I began writing. I had not written a poem since I was a youngster (although I was always very fond of it) and always made good grades in English and composition. I cannot explain how it occurred, except that someone or something (apparently it was my higher power) began guiding my hand along the paper until a four-verse poem was completed! It still amazes me because I had heard of things occurring like this, but it had never happened to me!

Once it was finished, I read and reread it to try and determine what the purpose was. Suddenly the title "Try My Friend" came to me because it was about my relationship with God as well as a challenge to others. What was so interesting about this verse was, four months later it won a Golden Globe award at the World of Poetry's International Convention in Las Vegas! Since that time, it has been put to music (once as a surprise by my girlfriend) and twice by recording industry people, however, I never pursued the publishing rights. It has also been included in many obituaries, publications, and recited at poetry readings.

That poem, written during my so-called "downtime," was the beginning of my writing career. After that time, I became so obsessed with the written word that I continued to write and enrolled in a two-year nonfictional writing course. I was so busy writing that some of my friends started worrying about me. Some even believed that I was ill or that I had a new boyfriend! I had simply revised my lifestyle, and most of my time was spent writing. (I was not as available as before via the telephone.)

I learned during that two-year period that at last, I had found my passion - the thing that brought me so much peace - the ability to express myself through the written word! What had happened during the quiet time was that I took the time to listen and was awakened to my gift! Since that initial poem, I have also written and self-published two poetry books, many essays, op-ed pieces, inspirational articles, and wrote a manual entitled, "How to Set up a Home-Based Medical Collection Agency."

We all have talents, however, being in abusive relationships will not allow for growth because you cannot express your creative self. In retrospect, I understand that I had this talent all the time, however, it could not surface because I was involved in so many "draining" (negative) relationships! When you cannot express yourself, your creativity will be suppressed, and many people become ill when their positive energy cannot surface. Although I do not profess to be a physician, it is my opinion (and that of many others) that many cancers and other illnesses evolve when one is unable to express themselves; in other words, when you body and mind are not in alignment, eventually you become ill. If you are continually performing "out of sync" with what your desires are; you are not being true to the Self! If you are constantly doing what someone else wants you to do, rather than what brings you peace and fulfillment; many people believe this causes stress which leads to illness!

There are many people who are probably saying, "I cannot write, act, sing, dance, or bake great cakes, etc." Maybe none of these appeal to you, but each person is born with talents, and some people have many. Do not allow anyone to denigrate those gifts by remaining in an abusive relationship where you are not free. That is your birthright!

The Right to Gainful Employment. Apparently, when I married my first husband, he was unfamiliar with the "Right to Work Laws" because he informed me that I should not get a job! Although I am saying this in a comical way, he literally attempted to prevent me from working.

I knew that I had the "right to gainful employment;" so I did not understand why I could not utilize my skills to help support our family. Initially I believed his concern was leaving our six-month old son but realized that was not the problem because my mother's best friend (our landlord and the person who lived upstairs) was going to keep him. I realized that was not his problem, and when I questioned him further, he said his mother never worked, and he did not believe a married woman was supposed to work outside of her home! I was outraged! My mother had always worked; even with my father working three jobs (a minister, a railroad maintenance worker, and having a part-time sales job in the evening) it was her choice, and he did not have a problem with it. Because my mother had a 10th grade education, she stressed the importance of obtaining an education. Our small town only had a junior college, which I completed prior to our marriage. (We met in college after he returned from the military, so he knew that I was not studying to be a housewife!)

    I asked the landlord to watch our son for a few hours while I went out to seek employment, stopping at the unemployment office first where I would apply for a secretarial position. After testing, they hired me to pay unemployment insurance. I was so excited, so when he came home, I thought he would also, because that would be extra money for our household. I shared the employment papers with him, hoping that he would change his mind, but he became very irate (another "red flag" which I missed)! In retrospect, I should have known he was an abuser because he was trying to exert control for no reason! Embarrassed as I am to say this, I desperately wanted, as so many women and men do, to make the relationship work because my mother had said that it would not work because she did not believe he was the right person! Secondly, I wanted it to work because my mother and father's relationship worked!

    Even though I was contributing to the family, he always resented my working, and he never liked any of the friendships I made (even though he would treat them cordially). I continued to work there, while he constantly referred to the job in a negative manner, because I knew that I had "birthright entitlements," and one of those was the right to earn a living. When my six months was up, I applied for a higher position as a medical transcriber for the State Department of Rehabilitation and remained there for four years until I left him, moving to California.

If someone adamantly tells you that you cannot go to work, and they do not have valid reasons, and it is your desire to do so; you probably have someone who is controlling, insecure, or jealous. If there are no overt reasons: he/she probably has an ulterior motive! (For example, my husband did not want me to find out about his womanizing!)

The Right to Freedom. The above-mentioned concept should truly be a part of this one. Your freedom is a precious entity! When you are limited or stifled, as reiterated earlier, you cannot be happy. When you are not functioning at your highest capacity, you will feel as if you are missing something. Some people describe this as an "emptiness."

People with low self-esteem are targets for abuse because they are continually seeking approval. Rather than developing their own inner strengths, they look for the outward. Many abused people who have not had therapy, or those who were abused as children, fall into this category. They seek people whom they believe will validate or like them. They get used over and over because they are so needy, requiring so much attention. Remain true to your integrity, in other words, you do not need someone to constantly stroke or give you approval!

Compliments should be appreciated, but if you are aware of who you are, and you are doing those things that bring you fulfillment, what another person says or believes about you will not be important! If you are feeling insecure or have the feelings described above, do get counseling so that you can exert your right to be free!

The Right to Change. There are many people who become unhappy or sever the relationship because the partner "empowers" him/herself. Several male respondents, as noted earlier, said they divorced their wives or partners after they went back to school or obtained a higher position at work because they were no longer compatible. Empowering or developing oneself should not be a threat or detriment in a relationship. Everyone should have the freedom to grow. When people deter you from this right, again, they have problems! Either they are suffering from a character or personality disorder, as discussed earlier.

Some men and women have denied their mate the right to change the style of their hair, or they have to dress a certain way; this is ludicrous! One of my respondents shared that his wife had long hair when he met her, however, she decided that it caused too much stress in her life, so she had it cut without consulting him. Because she would not let it grow again, he said he "fell out of love with her" and obtained a divorce. I was shocked at his response because he was an elderly man. Unless he gets help, he will be a controlling person to each woman he gets involved with.

It is understandable that one might like the mate's hair the way it was when they met, but to use this as a reason for the demise of a relationship shows overprotection, and is probably a signal that he/she is controlling other areas of the mate's life.

That is emotional abuse!

The Right to Be Selfish. This has been discussed in several of the other headings and is similar to one's right to be free or change. Briggs (referred to previously) says you must be true to yourself first to have power. "People pleasers" are popular. They make excellent friends because most are warm and nurturing, however, they have insecure personalities because they reach "outward" rather than "inward." In other words, they do not understand themselves, but they spend their time trying to help as well as to understand others! I must admit, prior to my healing, I was one of those "nice" people. Although there is an old adage, "It's nice to be nice," if you are constantly putting yourself at the end of your priority list, you will eventually become unhappy, ill, stressed, etc., because some of the time and energy you are expending on others should be spent with you!

You were born for you, and only you can claim your rightful inheritance, says Briggs. You are the designer of your world! For example, this was confirmed to me in a church service that I visited years ago. The minister said, "Whatever is going on in your life, you created it!" I thought, "He's out of his mind; I did not create those problems in my marriages, at work, or other problems I have had throughout my life!" As I listened further to his explanation, I realized that I had contributed by creating my world. This might sound foreign to some people, but I had a choice in my relationships, jobs, friendships, etc. When problems began, they were "red flags" which I ignored which were present to warn me that there was more to come! I, in all cases, ignored the signals and continued to pursue or allow future ones!

You cannot blame other people totally when relationships do not work, not to say that people are justified in their actions, but to assure you that you do have choices! You can be selfish (which is not what we were taught as children!) In my own case, I could have waited longer before marrying, asked more questions, etc., so that I would have known more. Instead, I was so impressed by outward appearances and superficialities. For example, it is very comical now, but my reasoning for marrying my first husband was that he was an excellent dancer, I loved to dance, and we danced well together! That was definitely no reason to marry or cohabit with him!

The minister (referred to previously) was trying to get the audience to understand the following: you have the power to choose, and if you choose wrongly, you also have the power to make a change; whether it is to seek help, to remain in the environment, or to leave! Most people, however, will make many excuses for staying, but they continue to complain and place the blame on another person! They never take responsibility for their unwise choices.

Another important fact to remember is; sometimes it is your perception of what happens that makes the difference! My perception might be entirely different from yours, and that is why some people leave when the abusive situation does not change, and others remain and justify their behavior. You can either be proactive by alleviating the situation when you see abuse, or you can be reactive by waiting until something happens and then respond, however, the latter is very toxic! If you are always involved in negative situations; then you are also contributing to the abuse. Be truthful to yourself first, admit your mistakes, and then take steps to change the situation.

Because many people blame others for their so-called shortcomings, they don't want to admit that they have also played a role. I am not saying that victims create the abuse they undergo, because certainly I did not! To clarify, in some situations you do not stop it because you are unable to recognize it, in other cases, you justify the violations by using other reasons for remaining, you become addicted or co-dependent; then you are a "willing" participant! The old adage: "a non-response is also a response" applies to these speakers' analogies. When the abuse continues, and you do nothing, in most occasions it worsens because both parties become addicted. The situation at that point resembles two alcoholics in a relationship!

People with high self-esteem nurture themselves. They do not give their powers away; however, people in abusive situations, who do not leave, allow others to make their decisions. I am not stating that your mate should not be involved in major decision making; what I am reiterating is, your personal happiness is your responsibility, not someone else's!

The Right to Your Own Values. You should be the person to establish your value systems. Children are unable to establish guidelines for themselves, so parents or another adult are responsible for this role. As an adult you should know what is right for you, so that you know what is proper for your children. Your mate might have one opinion about something, but you are entitled to have another about the same issue! This is the "right" that has caused so many couples to divorce. Hopefully, by the time that you decide to enter a serious relationship, your value systems, beliefs, etc. will have been discussed many times. Should you not be able to work these issues out, you should definitely get some marriage counseling or decide that there are too many differences to stay together.

Sometimes differences, however, are said to enrich a relationship, because there is diversity, but in some cases the differences will deter it. For example, if you are a Democrat, your spouse is a Republican, or you don't vote at all; if there is respect, love, and communication, etc., the relationship should not have problems. For example, there is a very famous political couple who appears frequently on <u>NBC's Meet the Press</u>, a very popular Sunday morning news show. He is Democrat, and she is Republican. When they appear, after debating, most people believe they are either going home to fight or get a divorce, however, according to reports, they are one of the happiest couples in the political arena! Apparently this couple understands that love, respect, communication, and freedom are the most important factors in their marriage, yet they are individuals who are free to adamantly disagree on issues, but it does not deteriorate the love they have for each other!

Allan F. Brimhall, in his article "Perfect Life Is Mine" wrote, "It is my birthright to enjoy life fully, joyfully, abundantly and in perfect health, as I experience the co-creation of all aspects of my life."

<u>The Right to Trust</u>. You have the right to trust only those people who deserve it.

Trust is a commodity that has to be earned. If people would treat others the way they desired to be treated, it would not include betrayal or abuse. Many of the respondents stated their relationships went sour because their partner could no longer be trusted; they were caught in lies, or the partner took them for granted, not treating them the way they did when they first met. Once this happens, marriage counseling and communication will have to be incorporated into the relationship, otherwise, it is probably "doomed."

  Jealousy is discussed in another chapter, however, this is one reason some people have problems with trust, and in many situations, these people were hurt, betrayed, or abused as a child or teen and did not get help. The other person will have to understand what the insecure person has been through, however, understanding jealousy should not be an excuse to be abusive, or allow abuse, into your relationship. Again, therapy will be required for the overly jealous mate.

  Some adults have not been trustworthy in raising children, so the children "pattern" them. There were some respondents that were still living with problems about trust because they were abused by a loved one. That is understandable, if you cannot trust those close to you, whom can you trust?

  Throughout my interviews, trust was one of the main reasons people were discontent. In fact, one woman said her younger sister slept with every man she was involved with: the husband and most of her boyfriends, consequently, she no longer trusts anyone! I understand her dilemma, however, that must be a dreadful way for anyone to live a lifetime, believing all people are bad. Society must break those cycles by educating and empowering so that victims of abuse can return to that state of innocence and openness which they were born with, and that applies to children and adults!

The Right to Your Own Feelings. "The devil made me do it," a popular saying that many used during the 50's (from a sitcom during that period) cannot be used because you have allowed someone to control your thoughts, and you respond in a negative manner! Do not allow anyone to have power over your emotions, so that you respond out of your normal behavior. You are responsible for how you respond to another person's negativity. (Remember the woman who is serving a life sentence because her husband had allegedly beat her for years?) Many people, after allowing abuse for years, will do something to retaliate against the abuser. For example, the man who stated he committed adultery for over 20 years (cited earlier) and the wife knew but never said anything; when he had a heart attack, she would not give him a glass of water or take him to the hospital. He said he almost died! Whether you agree or disagree with her response, she responded in an emotionally abusive manner because of his years of womanizing. Had she fought him while he was playing around, she might have been incarcerated.

You are just as responsible as the abuser if you are aware that someone is violating you, and you remain in the situation for other motives and suddenly "crack" after many years. Although a few people, after going to jail for murdering an abusive spouse, have been pardoned; in most cases, the judge, jury, etc., are not sure the alleged victim is telling the truth because the other person is dead, so the person is sent to prison! Even if the person was not killed, but you pulled a gun, fought, or rendered bodily injury to the abuser; in some cases, both of you are sent to jail. If there are children, they are sent to live with family or put in foster homes. So be aware that you do have the right to your own feelings, but if you stay with a person who harms you, and are pushed to suddenly respond, in most cases, authorities, jury, judges, etc., will also find you guilty!

The Right to Communicate. The University of California has developed a list of human rights called "Some (Commonly Denied) Human Rights" according to a report on the World Wide Web. For example, the right to ask for what you want, the right to offer no reason/excuse for your behavior (as long as it is not harmful to another person) and the right to say, "I don't know," to mention a few.

You would think the right to speak would be self-explanatory, but you would be surprised as to how many people divorce or end a relationship because one partner was not allowed to share or discuss anything. Each person should have the right to be heard. Counseling is advisable to couples having problems in this area.

We have previously discussed effective communication, and this refers to everyone. If someone whom you prefer to continue a relationship with talks in a demeaning way, you should let them know that you do not want to be spoken to in that manner. Should it continue, you are not being respected, and that refers to anyone: family member, friend, or associate.

If you are dating, yet constantly arguing, that is a signal that something needs to be fixed. Several respondents interviewed said their spouses had "sharp tongues," and it was the reason the relationship was destroyed. Even though you have the right to communicate, that does not mean that you are free to "talk down" to another person.

When someone constantly uses abusive language to you, it eventually becomes commonplace. For example, I do not understand why a woman would stay in a relationship with a man who refers to her as a "B....!" One woman told me she "just got used to it!" What would cause someone to become numb to a derogatory name, while still living as husband or wife, raising children, and supposedly sleeping together? Only a person with low self-esteem, a mental/emotional problem, or years of repeated abuse would allow someone to respond in that manner!

In summary, you have the right to be you! If you are unfamiliar with the above rights, it will take some time to implement them into your life. One word of caution, however, is that you must first analyze yourself to determine your strengths and weaknesses and to understand why you are contributing to the abuse by allowing it the relationship. Whatever decision you make, realize that changes do not happen overnight, that counseling might help, and it is never too late to begin your healing process. If your mate will not respond by agreeing to therapy, you will have to make a decision as to whether you want to remain with abuse. The key; however, is to recognize that there is a problem, get some help, and move on to "higher levels" - with or without the other person or persons!" Remember, your right to life includes the aforementioned birthright concepts, however, it is your choice as to whether you choose to enjoy them or not. According to Harriet Mohr, author of <u>What</u>

<u>the Soul Teaches</u>, says "Your body houses a higher power; treat it with respect and do not abuse it!

Each human being is unique and should be treated special. DNA molecules have proven these differences, and mathematicians have affirmed that it is impossible to make two people who are alike. You are a miracle! Do not allow abuse into your life - and as you continue to evaluate others, make sure that you are not harming another human being!

GLOSSARY*

There are some people who are in abusive situations because they do not understand the signals (as discussed previously) however; there are others who do not understand the various definitions. For example, many girls and boys believe rape means to be sexually violated by a stranger. That is not so! Even adult men and women are not clear on that issue. For example, one-fourth of female respondents and approximately 50% of males said people who put themselves in certain situations are asking to have sex, and the same number of men believed females "play games," when they say "no" but really mean "yes." We have included definitions, so that you are clear on what it means to be abused or abusive. In order to report assault, you must use the proper words, and it is most important that children express themselves clearly.

ASSAULT: All other physical attacks are prosecuted under assault

CHILD MOLEST: Willful committing of any lewd or lascivious act upon the child's body or any part or member of a child under 14-years old with the intent of arousing, appealing to, or gratifying the lusts, passions, or sexual desires of such person or child

INCEST: Sexual intercourse between blood relatives or surrogate family. The term has unofficially broadened in the field of therapy to include a trusting adult or anyone with a power advantage, mental or physical, over a child who betrays that trust in a sexual manner, verbally or non-verbally, covertly, or overtly.

PENETRATION: In prosecuting the crime of rape, you must have evidence of penetration (when the penis comes in contact with the vagina), or to insert any foreign object into the vagina.

RAPE: An act of sexual intercourse where the person does not give consent and is not married to the assailant. According to the UC Davis report the law further defines rape as:

1) the person is incapable of consent due to mental disease

2) the act is accomplished against a person's will by means of force or fear of immediate and unlawful bodily injury

3) the person cannot resist due to intoxicating, narcotic or anesthetic substances given by the accused;

4) the act is accomplished against the victim's will by threatening to retaliate in the future against the victim or other person; and

5) the victim is unconscious.

SEXUAL BATTERY: Any person who touches an intimate part of another person if that touching is against the will of the person touched and is for the purpose of sexual arousal, gratification or abuse. Intimate parts include sexual organs, groin, buttocks, and breasts.

SPOUSAL RAPE: Sexual intercourse against the victim's will by the spouse which does not force or fear of immediate accomplishes unlawful bodily harm or future retaliation. It must be reported within 90 days.

UNLAWFUL SEXUAL INTERCOURSE: An act of sexual intercourse (consensual or not) with a female under the age of 18 who is not your spouse.

*as defined by the UC Davis Internet report "Sexual Assault Terms."

ORGANIZATIONS

Listed below are organizations working in an effort to help in all areas of abuse. If you do not find a contact in your location, they will make references.

CHILD ABUSE AND NEGLECT:

Action for Child Protection
202 E. Street, NW
Washington, DC 20002
(202) 393-1990

American Humane Association
9725 East Hampden Avenue
Denver, CO 80231
(303) 695-0811

The American Professional Society on the Abuse of Children
969 E. 10th. Street
University of Chicago
Chicago, IL 60637
(213) 836-2471
An organization that seeks to bring together the professional disciplines for promoting improvements in the area of identification, assessment, and treatment of child victims, offenders, and family.

Catholic Children's Aid Society
(416) 925-6641

Child Welfare League of America
440 - lst. Street, N.W.
Washington, DC 20001
638-2952

The Child Help National Child Abuse Hot Line
Hot Line: 1-800-4-A-CHILD or (800) 422-4453
5757 N. 78th.
Scottsdale, AZ. 85260
Provides 24-hr crisis counseling, referrals, and information from professional counselors for all states 24 hours per day, 7 days a week

The Henry Kempe National Center for Prevention & Treatment of Child Abuse and Neglect
1205 Oneida Street
Denver, Colo. 80220
(303) 321-3963

Mothers Against Violence in America (MAVIA)
(800) 243-2565
(800) 897-7697 or (206) 323-2303

Founded in 1994, a nonprofit organization to prevent violence by and against children, to encourage investment in prevention before young people are affected by violence, and to advocate for changes that support a safer America for all children. They established 126 chapters of Students Against Violence Everywhere (SAVE) in elementary, middle, and high schools in 23 states.

To become a member, volunteer, to start a MAVIA or SAVE chapter; telephone the above numbers or see their website at www.mavia.org/volunteer.asp

National Center for Child Abuse and Neglect
P. O. Box 1182
Washington, D.C. 20013
(301) 251-5157

National Center for Missing and Exploited Children
1835 K Street, NW
Washington, DC 20006
(202) 634-9821
(703) 235-3900
Organized by John and Reve Walsh.
They are advocates for missing children, citings,
and sexual abuse as well as provide publications.
Website: www.missingkids.com receives more than
2 million hits per day.

National Committee for Prevention of Child Abuse
332 South Michigan Avenue
Chicago, IL 60604
(312) 663-3520

National Exchange Club Foundation for Prevention
of Child Abuse
3050 Central Avenue
Toledo, OH 43606
(419) 535-3232

National Network of Runaway and Youth Services
905 - 6th Street, NW
Washington, DC 20024
(202) 488-0739

The National Resource Center on Child Sexual
Abuse
11141 Georgia Avenue, Suite 310
Wheaton, MD 20902
(301) 949-5000
Information, training, and technical assistance.

Parents Anonymous
7120 Franklin Avenue

Los Angeles, CA 90046
421-0353

Parents Television Council
P. O. Box 7802
Burbank, CA. 91510-9817
Organized to stop violence, vulgarity, etc. in television. They accept tax-exempt contributions for advertisements, etc.

Parents United/Daughters and Sons United/Adults Molested as Children United
P. O. Box 952
San Jose, CA 95108
(408) 280-5055
National self-help groups for families with sexual abuse problems. They sponsor groups throughout the country for children, teens, parents, and adults molested as children.

Sexual Assault Crisis Center
Knoxville, TN.
(423) 522-7273

DOMESTIC VIOLENCE:

Batterers Anonymous
8485 Tamarind, Suite D
Fontana, CA. 92335
(714) 355-1100

Center for Women's Policy Studies
Tacoma, Washington
Short-term residential treatment program for batterers - 4 week program center for Women

Center for Women Policy Studies
2000 P. Street, N.W. Suite 508
Washington, D.C. 20036
(202) 871-1770
Established in 1972 to conduct research. Provides information about family violence and sexual violence against women.

The Family Violence Prevention Fund
(415) 252-8900.
A nonprofit organization dedicated to eliminating domestic violence. Offers referral services for counseling, legal, and housing services for survivors.

The Health Resource Center on Domestic Violence
383 Rhode Island Street, Suite 304
San Francisco, CA. 94103-5133
Toll free: (888) Rx-ABUSE
Email: fund@igc.apc.org
Web: http://www.fvpf.org/fund/
A project of the Family Violence Prevention Fund that provides training materials, technical assistance, information, and referrals to health care professionals and others serving victims of domestic violence.

National Coalition against Domestic Violence
1728 N. Street, N.W. Suite 201
Washington, D.C. 20036
(202) 544-7358

The National Coalition against Domestic Violence
2401 Virginia Avenue, N.W., Suite 306
Washington, D.C. 20037
(202) 293-8860

National Domestic/Abuse Hot Line
839-1852 (Denver)
(800) 799-7233 - 24 hour Hot Line
They provide information and referrals for shelters, counseling for adults and children, and assistance in reporting abuse. They have a 24-hour access to translators for approximately 150 languages. These resources are available to men, women, and children.

W.O.M.A.N., Inc.
San Francisco, California
(415) 864-4722
Offers legal assistance to battered women who seek protection through restraining orders in San Francisco, and provides guidance with self-representation in court, and follow-up of police responses. They have a 24-hour crisis line, bi-monthly, evening, and legal clinics.

The Women's Foundation
340 Pine Street, Suite 302
San Francisco, CA. 94102
(415) 837-1113
(415) 837-1144 (fax)
The oldest and largest philanthropic organization for women in the West provides training in policy action. They have been in force for 20 years, conducted a five-year study on the treatment of women and girls in California. To request a copy of the "California Report Card" which is $5.00, for information about the Foundation, or to be on the mailing list, write or email info@twfusa.org. Website: www.twfusa.org

ELDERLY:

Clearinghouse on Abuse and Neglect of the Elderly (CANE)
Department of Consumer Studies
University of Delaware
Newark, DE 19716
They are requesting training manuals, curriculum guides, publications, videotapes, etc. Share your materials with the Clearinghouse so that others can learn from, and about, you.

Commission on Legal Problems of the Elderly
740 - 15th. Street, N.W.
Washington, D.C. 20005
(202) 662-8692
(202) 663-8698 (fax)
For additional information to network with other professionals working in this area, join the Internet listserve or Email: lstiegel@staff.abanet.org.

Domestic Violent Internet Project
www.growing.com/nonviolent
The site, sponsored by Santa Clara County, has over 1,200 links to other websites related to domestic violence, a 4,000-item bibliography, with 38 books on elder abuse.

Elderly Services Partnership Coalition
(510) 536-4162

WISE Senior Services
1527 Fourth Street, Suite 250
Santa Monica, CA. 90401
(310) 394-9871
(310) 395-4090 (fax)

email: saziz@wiseseniorservices.org or mfindler@wiseseniorservices.org

Los Angeles County Area Agency on Aging Fiduciary Abuse (FAST) established in 1993 to combat the rising number of elder financial abuse claims. Provides consultation to caseworkers and others assisting victims of elder financial abuse.

Multipurpose Senior Services Program
City of Oakland
(510) 238-3931

National Association of State Units on Aging
1225 I. Street, N.W. Suite 725
Washington, D.C. 20002-4267

National Center on Elder Abuse
1225 I. Street, N.W., Suite 725
Washington, D.C. 20005
(202) 898-2586
(202) 898-2583 (fax)
Email: NCEA@nasua.org

National Center on Elder Abuse
c/o American Public Welfare Association
810 First Street, N.E., Suite 500
Washington, D.C. 20002-4267
Provides elder abuse information to professionals and the public, offers technical assistance and training to elder abuse agencies and related professionals, conducts short-term research, and assists with elder abuse program and policy development.

National Committee for the Prevention of Elder Abuse
119 Belmont Street
Worcester, MA. 01605

Ombudsman, Inc.
1212 Broadway, #606
Oakland, CA. 94612-1824
(510) 465-1065
They consist of men and women of all ages who are trained volunteers who advocate for the rights of individuals in both skilled nursing facilities and residential care facilities. They receive and resolve complaints, mediate grievances, monitor conditions of care, protect residents' rights and find solutions to problems while stressing dignity for the aged.
They need volunteer advocates.

San Francisco Consortium for Elder Abuse Prevention
Goldman Institute on Aging
3330 Geary Blvd.
San Francisco, CA. 94118
(415) 750-4188
(415) 750-4136 (fax)
A 29-page technical assistance manual produced by the National Center on Elder Abuse entitled "Victims' Rights and Services: Assisting Elderly Crime Victims" can be purchased from the Consortium for $15.00. (8.5% tax for orders shipped within California). It is a necessary tool for anyone working with the elderly, to understand victims' roles, right, and special needs. You can also report financial abuse to the District Attorney's Office's, Elder Abuse Unit in your area.

GAY AND LESBIAN:

Community United Against Violence (CUAV)
333-HELP
Offers services specifically related to domestic-violence cases involving lesbians, gay men, bisexuals, transgender, and transsexual people. Services include counseling, support groups, and help getting temporary restraining orders.

Gay & Lesbian Alliance against Defamation (GLAAD)
1360 Mission Street, Suite 200
San Francisco, CA. 94103
(415) 861-2244

Gay & Lesbian Community Forum
America Online
Consists of four conference rooms, 23 message boards, over 40 libraries. There are over 40,000 members. They provide resources on HIV/AIDS, are a clearinghouse for ideas.

National Center for Lesbian Rights
870 Market Street, Suite 570
San Francisco, CA. 94102
(415) 392-6257

National Lesbian and Gay Crisis Line
(800) 221-7044

Youth Crisis
(415) 621-2929

INCEST:

The Incest Recovery Association
6200 North Central Expressway, Suite 209
Dallas, TX 75206
(214) 373-6607
Nonprofit organization. Provides information and treatment for victims of incest.

The Incest Survivor Information Exchange
P. O. Box 3399
New Haven, CT. 06515
(203) 389-5166
Quarterly newsletter with a theme related to sexual abuse. Confidential mailing list.

Survivors of Incest Anonymous
P. O. Box 21817
Baltimore, MD 21222
(301) 282-3400
A mutual-help group, guided by the 12-step and traditions of AA. They are made up of men and women 18 years of age or older. 24-hour telephone service.

Voices in Action, Inc.
(Victims of Incest Can Emerge Survivors)
P. O. Box 148309
Chicago, IL 60614
(312) 327-1500
Publishes a newsletter, offers a survival kit that includes a bibliography and information on how to choose a therapist, how to start a self-help group, and also organizes conferences. They have special interest groups made up of all types of people; multiple personalities, anorexic/bulimic, lesbians,

victims of post-traumatic stress, self-abuse, all abuse survivors, etc.

MALES:

Basic Training for Boys
P. O. BOX 9525
Oakland, CA. 94613
This group empowers young boys by teaching them to be self-sufficient. They also have a "how-to" videotape on making a bed, tying a tie, etc., and have received many awards for their work from various parents and magazines as well as other national publications. The tape is $14.95 plus $3.95 shipping.

EMERGE: A Men's Counseling Service on Domestic Violence
18 Hurley Street, Suite 23
Cambridge, MA. 02141
(617) 422-1550
Seeks to end male violence against women by helping batters to explore the causes of their violence and to find alternatives. Offers community workshops and classes on the abuse of women from a male perspective.

Harvard Anti-Sexist Men (HASM)
c/o Student Activities Office
108 Longfellow Hall
Appian Way
Cambridge, MA. 02138
Founded in 1991 to encourage men to take responsibility for sexism and male violence against women and to challenge traditional concepts of masculinity.

Men for Change
5500 Inglis Street (Unitarian Church Hall)
Halifax, Nova Scotia, Canada
492-4104 (for information)
This organization has worked since 1989 to end sexism, violence, and to promote gender equality. They are male positive, pro-feminist, and gay affirmative. They have a resource catalog called "Men Changing Men." Meetings are held every third Tuesday at 7:00 p.m.

Men's Rights, Inc.
P. O. Box 163180
Sacramento, Ca. 95816
(916) 484-7333
Men's Rights is dedicated to ending sexism and to correct the social and economical inconsistencies involving men. They believe that women are as likely as men to initiate violence within relationships and the "The Battered Woman's Defense" is a sexist term that should be replaced with "The Battered Person's Defense." They publish a newsletter, "New Release" along with position papers and articles. Staffed totally by volunteers.

National Center for Fathering
P. O. Box 413888
Kansas City, MO. 64141
(800) 593-DADS
For information on training, tapes, or other resources:
(800) 593-3237, X-18

The National Center for Men, Oregon Chapter
P.O. Box 6481

Portland, OR 97228-6481
224-9477
E-mail: ncmen@teleport.com
Web page: www.teleport.com/-ncmen/index.htm
They have a quarterly newsletter entitled <u>The Equalist Review</u>, $16.00/year, not tax deductible and a newsletter, Men's Right's Report. Counseling services are free.

Oakland Men's Project
1203 Preservation Parkway
Oakland, CA. 94612
(510) 465-1800 or (510) 835-2433
Hotline: 800-924-1070.
Referrals to batterers' intervention and workshops for boys and men to eliminate sex-role stereotyping as well as to eliminate abuse towards females.

Prevention, Leadership, Education, and Assistance
P. O. Box 291182
Los Angeles, CA. 90029
(213) 254-9962
Nonprofit organization for non-offending adult male survivors of childhood sexual, physical, or emotional abuse. It is also open to pro-survivors such as partners, friends, family members, clergy, and all other individuals who care for or about the male survivor.

TAB - Therapy for Abusive Behavior
Baltimore, MD.
Men must participate in TAB's Program as an alternative to further legal action, by the Judge.

VIBS
Long Island, New York

Couples counseling. When men believe they are going to abuse wives, they call the hot line instead.

RAPE:

Bay Area Women against Rape
(510) 845-7273
24-hr rape crisis center, hot line counseling, advocacy through medical/legal systems, short-term in-person counseling, and community education.

RAINN (Rape, Abuse, Incest National Network)
Hot line
252 - 10th. Street, NE
Washington, D.C. 20002
656-HOPE
It's free and confidential.

Rape Crisis Center
(510) 237-0113
Individual therapy for women, teens, and children of sexual assault and their families, group therapy sessions, 24-hr crisis line, medical/legal and advocacy, girls' assertiveness/self-defense training, community education, speaker's bureau, and prevention workshops.

San Francisco Women against Rape
(415) 647-RAPE
Offers counseling service 24 hours a day, seven days a week. Counseling services are offered in ten different languages.

Stop Prisoner Rape
333 North Avenue 61, #4

Los Angeles, CA. 90042
(213) 257-6164
(For information requests or to contribute, e-mail: information@spr.)

SEX ADDICTIONS:

Co-dependents to Sex Addiction
P. O. Box 14537
Minneapolis, MN 55414
(612) 537-6904
For people who are in or have been in a relationship with a sex addict.
Sex and Love Addicts Anonymous
P. O. Box 88
New Town Branch, Boston, MA 02258
For people who are sexually compulsive or obsessive about romantic relationships.

Adult Children of Sex Addicts
P. O. Box 8084, Lake Street Station
Minneapolis, MN 55408
For people who were raised in sexually addictive or dysfunctional families.
"What is Sex Addiction?" (Mic Hunter)

Hazeldon Foundation Educational Materials
Box 176
Center, City, MN 55012-0176
(800) 328-9000
They have material on sex addiction, alcoholics, chemical dependents, co-dependents, and adult children of troubled or dysfunctional families.

S-ANON I.F.G. (Sexaholics Anonymous International Family Groups)

P. O. Box 111242
Nashville, Tenn. 37222-1242
12-step fellowship of people affected by the sexual addiction of a family member or friend. There are no dues or membership fees. For more information send $1 check or money order, no cash) to cover postage and handling.

LEGAL ASSISTANCE:

The San Francisco Legal Assistance Foundation
(415) 981-1300.
Offers a cooperative restraining order clinic by appointment once a week. Representation is available for low-income residents of San Francisco in eight languages.

The San Francisco Bar Association
(415) 982-8416.
Offers a cooperative restraining order clinic for women who qualify under the Domestic Violence Protection Act. A staff attorney is available to take women through the process of getting a restraining order. Services available in Spanish and English.

Nihonmachi Legal Outreach
(415) 567-6255.
A nonprofit legal organization that helps battered Asian and Pacific Islanders in a variety of languages. Services are offered on a sliding scale and are free to those on public assistance.

The Riley Center
415) 255-0165.
Offers emergency shelter for battered women and their children, as well as long-term transitional

housing. Services include peer counseling, referrals, children's counseling, and case-management advocacy.

MISCELLANEOUS:

Adults Molested as Children United
P. O. Box 952
San Jose, CA. 95108
(408) 280-5055
A mutual-help group that is an outgrowth of Parents United.

Community Health Center, Inc.
P. O. Box 1076
Middletown, CT. 96457
347-6971
All have national newsletters at no cost.

Doris Tate Crime Victims Foundation
Court Watch Program
915 L. Street, Suite 1120
Sacramento, Ca. 95814
(800) 7-Victims (784)-2846
(916) 556-1237
A nonprofit organization designed to increase victim awareness. The Court Watch program was designed to inform the public about local judges, hold them accountable for their actions, and acknowledge those judges who deserve recognition for outstanding service.

The National Organization for Victim Assistance
717 D. Street, NW, Suite 200
Washington, D.C. 20004
(202) 393-NOVA

Addresses victims and co-victims of crime of all types. They organize public campaigns to protest victimization.

National Victim/Witness Resource Center
108A South Columbus Street
Alexandria, VA 22314

National Victims Resource Center
Box 6000
Rockville MD 120850
(800) 627-6872
Established in 1983 by the U. S Department of Justice's Office for Victims of Crime. NVRC is crime victims' primary source of information. The center answers questions by using national and regional statistics, a comprehensive collection of research findings, and a well-established network of victim advocates and organizations.

Oakland Healthy Start
9925 E. 14th. Street, Suite 11
Oakland, CA. 94603
(510) 437-8970
They provide services for children and families.

Referral Service of San Francisco Chapter of
California Association of Marriage
and Family Therapists
(415) 441-5644
They can help you select a trained therapist following crisis.

Safer Society Press
3049 East Genesee Street
195

Syracuse, NY 13224
(315) 455-6748

YWCA of the USA
Local YWCA's provide a wide range of programs and services, including battered women's shelters and counseling, child care, support to victims of rape and sexual assault, job training, health, and advocacy, etc.
Toll free (888) YWCA-INFO (national information line for your local YWCA)

SEXUAL HARASSMENT/WORKPLACE ISSUES:

Equal Rights Advocates
1663 Mission Street
San Francisco, CA. 94103
(800) 839-4ERA (bilingual advice and counseling hot line)
(415) 621-0672
A non-profit public interest law firm that helps protect women's rights in the work place.

STATE OFFICES:

Department of Social Services
Department of Human Services
Office of Child Abuse Prevention
Child Protective Services
Department of Health and Welfare
Department of Health and Human Resources
Division of Youth and Family Services
Department of Public Welfare
Department of Institutions, Social and Rehabilitation Services -

Division of Child Welfare
Department of Children and Families

WEB SITES FOR SUPPORT: (Essence, July 1997).

National Victim Center
(http://www.nvc.org)
Leads on how and where to get help in your region on prevention information and links to resourceful sites.

Counseling
(http://www.counseline.com)
Chat with certified abuse counselors for a fee ($25 for 25 minutes) or get responses to specific questions via E-mail.

The Sanctuary
(http://avocado.wustl.fu/-chack/sanct/sanctuary.html).
Refuse for victims of various types of abuse. Users share solutions and inspiration.

Santa Clara County websites on violence:
www.growing.com/nonviolent
(See their site for handbook for victims with 1,200 links to other websites related to domestic violence, elder abuse, resources for battered men, Asian domestic violence resources, workplace violence, etc.)

HOTLINES:*

Child Abuse Hot line   (800) 4-A-CHILD
Child Support Hot line (800) 252-3515

Depression Hot line   (800) 551-0008
Gay & Lesbian Youth (800) 347-TEEN
National Center for   (800) 843-5678
  Missing and Exploited Children
Parents Anonymous - Abuse

*(See New York Public Library citation)

BIBLIOGRAPHY

Abuse Intervention Project, World Wide Web, America Online, May 21, 1997.

Ackerman, Diane, "The Fears that Save Us," Parade.

Aronson, Tara, "Who Will Save the Children?" Santa Clara County Study Shows Troubles Inherent in Our Family Court System," San Francisco Examiner & Chronicle, March 16, 1997.

Authelet, Emil, Jr., (Dr.), Parenting Solo, Here's Life Publishers, San Bernardino, 1989.

Babich, Phillip, "Spousal Abuse & Child Abuse Are Two Sides of the Same Coin," Express, October 17, 1997, p. 3.

Bender, David, et al, Violence Against Women, Greenhaven Press, Inc., San Diego, CA., 1994.

"Bishop Sex Tape," The Oakland Tribune, October 2, 1999, p. 2.

Briggs, Dorothy Corkille, Celebrate Yourself: Enhancing Your Own Self-Esteem, Doubleday, New York, 1977.

Brimhall, Allan F., "Perfect Life is Mine, Science of Mind, Spokane, WA., 1997.

"Brothers Found Chained to Beds," <u>Los Angeles Sentinel</u>, October 19-25, 2000, A-17.

Brown, Carl, <u>Abuse from My Mind: A Book of Poetry to Ease Your Mind</u>, Brown Palace Publications, San Lorenzo, California, 1997.

The California Wellness Foundation, "AIDS and Cancer Aren't the Only Diseases We Need to Conquer," <u>The Oakland Tribune</u>, June 12, 1997, p. B-7.

"Child Predator Must Be Stopped," <u>Los Angeles Times</u>, December 11, 2000, p, E-5.

"Child Sexual Abuse," The Sexual Assault Crisis Center of Knoxville, TN., <u>World Wide Web, America Online</u>, May 21, 1997.

Chopra, Deepak, M.D., <u>Ageless Body Timeless Mind</u>, Harmony Books, N.Y., 1993.

"Common Questions About Abusers and Intervention Programs," From Kaiser Permanente's Report; "Domestic Violence Facts for Women," <u>World Wide Web, America Online</u>, May 21, 1997.

"Court Deems Child Abuse Story Reliable,"

The Oakland Tribune, Associated Press, December 30, 1997.

Cunningham, T., "Boyfriend Guilty in Baby Shaking," The Oakland Tribune, October 29, 1999, L5.

"Cycles of Nonviolence," Domestic Abuse Intervention Project, Duluth, MN., WOMAN, Inc., 1996, World Wide Web, America Online, May 21, 1997.

Davis, Karen, "Abused Teen Girls Likely to Face Host of Other Troubles," The Parsons Sun, October 1, 1997.

De Becker, Gavin, "The Dangerous Men," Glamour, 1997, p. 208.

De Becker, Gavin, The Gift of Fear: Survival Signals That Protect Us from Violence, Little Brown & Co., June, 1997.

De Becker, Gavin, Protecting the Gift: Keeping Children and Teenagers Safe (and Parents Sane), Dell Books, reprint May 2000.

Domestic Violence - Doesn't Stay at Home when a Woman Gets to Work, Blue Shield of California, San Francisco, CA., Colorado Domestic Violence Coalition, 1991.

"Domestic Violence Under-Reported - Nearly Half of Victims Knew Their Attackers," Parsons Sun, August 25, 1997, p. 1.

"Early Signs for Future Abuse," from "When Battered Women Kill," The Free Press, New York, 1987, Distributed by The Duluth Domestic Abuse Intervention Project WOMAN, Inc., 1996, World Wide Web, America Online, May 21, 1997.

Elsner, Alan, "Pedophiles," America Online, February 22, 2001.

Gardiner, Lisa, "Ex-Pastor Faces New Molesting Charge," The Oakland Tribune, November 10, 1999, p. L-6.

Gelles, Richard J. & Murray A. Straus, Intimate Violence - The Definite Study of the Causes and Consequences of Abuse in the American Family, Simon and Schuster, New York, 1988.

"General Statistics," Family Violence Prevention Fund, Newsflash, World Wide Web, America Online, January 1997.

"Gordon, Marilyn, Healing is Remembering Who You Are: A Guide for Healing Your Mind, Your Emotions, and Your Life, Robert D. Reed, San Francisco, 1995.

"Grandfather Convicted of Molestation," WAVE Newspapers, August 23, 2000, p. 6.

Gregory, Deborah, "Who Is That Man," Essence, February 1997, p. 138.

"The Health Care Response to Domestic

Violence," (compiled from numerous individual studies; 1987-1985), Family Violence Prevention Fund, <u>America Online,igc.apc.org/fund/the-facts/health-response</u>, May 21, 1997.

Health ResponseAbility Systems, Inc., 1995, <u>World Wide Web, America Online</u>, November 16, 1996.

Herman, Judith Lewis, <u>Trauma and Recovery: The Aftermath of Violence</u>, 1993.

Holtz, H.A., "The Health Care Response to Domestic Violence, reprinted by WOMAN, Inc., <u>World Wide Web, America Online</u>, May 21, 1997.

Hopper, Jim, Ph.D., Child Abuse: Statistics, Research, and Resources," www. <u>Jimhopper.com/,AmericaOnline</u>, 9/24/98.

Hubner, John and Jill Wolfson, <u>Somebody Else's Children</u>, Crown, New York, 1996.

"Infant Brain Damage Affected Morals in Two Test Subjects," <u>The Oakland Tribune</u>, October 19, 1999, N5.

Inform Editor, Congressional Caucus for Women's Studies, inform-editor@ umail.umd.edu., <u>World Wide Web, America Online</u>, January 14, 1997.

Kaufman, Barry, Neil, "Happiness is a Choice," <u>Creative Thought</u>, Vol. 78, #1,

January,1997, p. 22.

Langan, P. A., et al, "Preventing Domestic Violence Against Women," National Crime Survey, World Wide Web, America Online, May 21, 1997.

Marecek, Mary, Breaking Free from Partner Abuse, Morning Glory Press, Buena Park, CA. 1993.

"Man Gets Five Years for Cyber Affair with Teenager," Parsons Sun, August 23, 1997, p. 7.

McManus, Michael J., "Become a Marriage Saver," World Wide Web, America Online Online, November 7, 1996.

McManus, Michael J., Helping Your Friends and Family Avoid Divorce, Zondervan Publishing House, Rev. 1998.

Miller, G., "Violence By and Against America's Children," Journal of Juvenile Justice Digest, XVII, 1989, p. 12.

Mohr, Harriet, What the Soul Teaches, New Focus Press, Menlo Park, California, 1994.

"Molester Gets Five Years," The Oakland Tribune, November 13, 1999.

"Mother Serving Life Sentence for Son Raped by Pit Bull," PACE NEWS, Vol. 6, No. 2, November 10, 1000, p. 1.

"New Bill Requires Reporting of Sex Crimes," (Associated Press, AOL) Las Vegas Review Journal, September 10, 1998.

"New Crime Statistics," The National Resource Center on Domestic Violence, January, World Wide Web, America Online, Org/fund/materials/speakup/news/97, May 21, 1997.

Norwood, Robin, Women Who Love Too Much When You Keep Wishing and Hoping He'll Change, Pocket Books (Simon & Schuster), New York, 1985.

"Parents Held in Two Separate Cases of Infant Killings," The Los Angeles Times, May 24, 2000, B4.

"Parents Television Council," Oakland Tribune, 2/26/98.

Peck, M. Scott, M.D., The Road Less Traveled: A New Psychology of Love, Traditions, Values and Spiritual Growth, Simon & Schuster, New York, 1978.

Peled, Einat, et al, "Ending the Cycle of Violence: Community Responses to Children of Battered Women," via World Wide Web, America Online, May 21, 1997. (Sage Publishers, Thousand Oaks, Ca., 1996, 1994).

"Recovered Memories of Sexual Abuse: Scientific Research & Scholarly Resources," Jim Hopper, Ph.D., http://www.jimhopper.com/, America Online,7/24/98.

Roberts, Albert R., D.S.W., Beverly J. Roberts, M. Ed., Nancy A. Humphreys, D.S.W., Sheltering Battered Women: A National Study & Service Guide, Springer Publishers Company, New York, New York, 1981.

Robertson, Blair Anthony, "Net Stings: New Wave in Police Work," San Francisco Examiner, October 3, 1999, p. C-1.

Roget's International Thesaurus, 4th Edition, Harper & Row, New York, 1977.

"Safety Plan," WOMAN, Inc., 1996, World Wide Web, America Online, May 21, 1997.

"Some Sex Offenders Seek Controversial Procedure," Los Angeles Times, March 2, 2001, A-32, 33.

Sprague, Gary A., "How to Keep Family Dysfunction from Claiming the Next Generation," and "Breaking the Cycle," World Wide Web, America Online, November 7, 1996.

Straus, M.A. & R. J. Gelles, (eds.), Physical Violence in American Families, Transaction

Publishers, New Brunswick, N.J., 1990.

"TV Is Leading Children Down a Moral Sewer - How You and I Can Stop It," The Oakland Tribune, October 22, 1999, S12.

Webster's New World Dictionary of the American Language, 1968.

Whitfield, Charles L., M.D., Healing the Child Within, Health Communications, Inc., Deerfield Beach, FL., 1987, reprinted 1989.

"Why Don't Women Leave," WOMAN, Inc., 1996, http://www.cybersf.com/womaninc/why.html, America Online, May 21, 1997.

Williams, Samuel, Jr., "Killed Boyfriend: Battered Woman Pardoned after 15 Years in Prison," Los Angeles Sentinel, p. A-3.

Williamson, Kathy, "Davis Signs Iverson Child Victim Protection Bill," Los Angeles Sentinel, September 21, 2000, A-3.

Williamson, Marianne, A Woman's Worth, Ballantine Books, New York, 1993.

Winokur, Scott and Tyche Hendricks, "Antioch Mom, Son Accused of Felony Incest; Could Face Prison," San Francisco Examiner, November 7, 1999, C-10.

"Women Veterans' Experiences with Domestic

Violence and with Sexual Assault While In the Military: A New Study," Family Violence Prevention Fund, Women Veterans and Domestic Violence, <u>World Wide Web, America Online</u>, May 21, 1997.

"Women's Network," Congressional Caucus for Women's Issues, Federal Programs to Address Violent Crimes, <u>World Wide Web, America Online</u>, January 14, 1997.

Zukav, Gary, <u>The Seat of the Soul</u>, Simon & Schuster, New York, 1990, Zukav, lst Edition, 1989.

ABOUT THE AUTHOR

Gloria Edmonson-Nelson, mother of three adult sons and Grandmother of five, has always been concerned with humankind - especially children. This book evolved from the anthology she wrote and self-published in 1998; entitled <u>Recognizing Abuse: Reclaiming Your Birthright</u>, that discusses many types of abuse and shares steps for healing.

Research has shown when adults are involved in domestic violence or other types of abuse, if there are children in the home; they are victims. This book was written to help parents, family members, administrators and teachers, ministers; (anyone dealing with children and teens) understand the signals of abuse. Secondly, it is written to reiterate to adults that: "Any type of violence in your lives will perpetuate violence in the lives of your children!"

We must now be proactive as a society to take steps to stop what we have been doing so children will have a chance to live healthy lifestyles. We must also expose all pedophiles - no matter who they are!

Gloria is a graduate of the University of San Francisco with a management degree in human relations - organizational behavior. She completed the NRI School of Writing, Washington, D.C., in 1992, and began writing poetry and has written several books. She has written many articles and op ed pieces for various newspapers and newsletters and well as spiritual and inspirational books. (Please see List of Books in the appendix or visit Amazon.com).

She has worked in varied capacities: administrator of Far West Laboratory for

Educational Research and Development, S.F., medical malpractice reporter - The Doctors' Company, Emeryville, CA., securities arbitrator - NASD, S.F., and medical transcriber, etc.

She has volunteered with the United Way of the Bay Area, Hands Across the Golden Gate Bridge for the Homeless, West Angeles Skid Row Program, and many other projects.

Her hobbies are writing and traveling. Her most recent trip was to Nigeria and Ghana, Africa, with Save Africa's Children (a project developed by West Angeles Church, Los Angeles) in 2006, where she visited orphanages owned by SAC. Her concern for children and support for this project led her to accompany this group of 40. Touched by what she saw - she will continue to assist this project with funds from the sale of this book.

It is her desire that you will help all children of our nation - they are our future!

www.ingramcontent.com/pod-product-compliance
Lightning Source LLC
Chambersburg PA
CBHW061301110426
42742CB00012BA/2011